natural crochet
for babies & toddlers

natural crochet
for babies & toddlers

tina barrett

GUILD OF MASTER
CRAFTSMAN PUBLICATIONS

First published 2008 by

Guild of Master Craftsman Publications Ltd.
Castle Place, 166 High Street,
Lewes, East Sussex BN7 1XU

Text and designs © Tina Barrett, 2008

© in the Work GMC Publications, 2008

ISBN 978-1-86108-624-2

Associate Publisher **Jonathan Bailey**
Production Manager **Jim Bulley**
Managing Editor **Gerrie Purcell**
Project Editor **Virginia Brehaut**
Managing Art Editor **Gilda Pacitti**
Photographer **Chris Gloag**

Set in Avant Garde and American Typewriter

Colour origination by GMC Reprographics
Printed and bound by Kyodo Nation Printing in Thailand

contents

PART THREE

Accessories

PART FOUR

Crochet basics

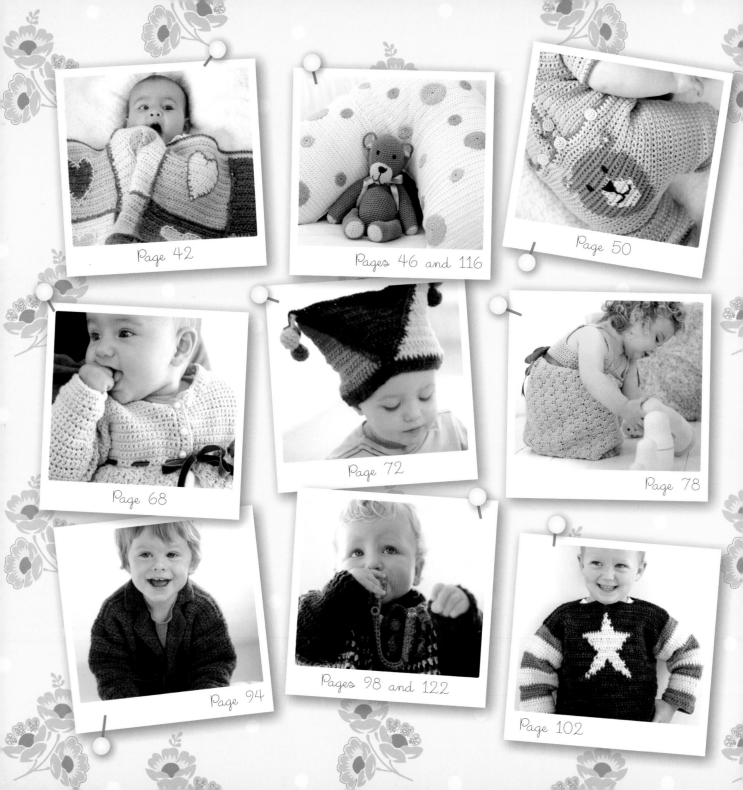

Page 42

Pages 46 and 116

Page 50

Page 68

Page 72

Page 78

Page 94

Pages 98 and 122

Page 102

introduction

When writing *Natural Knits for Babies & Toddlers*, the sister book to this, I wrote of how my inspiration came from the birth of my fourth child, Lily. With a sixteen-year age gap between Lily and my eldest daughter, it was quite a surprise to be expecting again! Now, two years on – after we had long gotten over the shock and fallen in love with Lily's gorgeous brown curls and infectious giggles, I am still as passionate as ever when it comes to designing beautiful children's toys and garments using only the finest quality, natural fibres.

From that point of view, this book is exactly the same as the last. Twenty gorgeous designs using only natural fibres, processed in the most gentle, organic way which will leave only a baby-sized eco footprint on the world after they have been produced. The only difference is that the eagle-eyed amongst you will have spotted that this is in fact a crochet book. If you are a seasoned crocheter, or even a beginner, then this book is ideal for you and I really hope you find pleasure in working through some of the featured projects.

However, if you see yourself as only a knitter, then I seriously urge you to read through the 'basics' section at the back and just have a go. Crochet is a wonderfully portable and satisfying craft and really quite simple to pick up once you've got the hang of things. I assure you, it won't be long before you are well and truly hooked!

I really hope these pages inspire you and that you find something wonderful within them to crochet for your little miracle. And, just like I told you in the first book, everyone who has contributed to this book has taken good care of the bigger picture, all you need take care of now are the stitches themselves.

Happy crocheting,

Tina Barrett

natural yarns & fibres

If you are reading this book then you are probably a fan of natural fibres already. But in case you are undecided about their benefits, I am now going to give you a couple of fantastic reasons for at least giving them a go.

The first and eminently most sensible reason for using natural yarns is your baby's precious skin. A baby's skin is soft, sensitive and gorgeous (and very kissable). Therefore, it makes perfect sense to choose soft, natural, breathable fibres to put next to it. By that, I mean fibres that won't irritate and haven't been treated with harsh dyes or processed with chemicals. Natural organic yarns tick all these boxes so are the perfect choice for little ones. And your skin is precious too. Many of us grown-ups suffer with eczema, psoriasis and other skin problems. Contrary to popular belief, natural fibres are often perfect for those with allergies and sensitive skin. There is a natural fibre for everyone as I will outline later.

A second reason for choosing natural yarns is that they come from sustainable sources. They do not kill the animal or plant they are taken from and they avoid the use of artificial fertilizers, herbicides, fungicides or organo-phosphate dips, they can be produced with minimal pollution and therefore have a very low impact on the surrounding environment. So that's excellent news for the health of the planet and for the children we're crocheting for too!

Finally, natural yarns no longer break your bank. They are becoming more widely appreciated by everyone involved in the industry and are now being produced by larger yarn companies whose prices come in at about the same level as other fancy and man-made yarns. So now there's no excuse for not trying natural fibres.

I have chosen a combination of plant and animal fibres. Some of these may seem a little unusual and not part of your regular stash, so I will try to give you a little information about each so you know what to expect. They all differ in texture and drape and are well worth experimenting with as the eco-yarn revolution is only set to grow.

Soya

This yarn is made from 100% soya bean fibre and I can tell you now it is incredibly smooth, has a silky handle in fabric and is 100% natural in origin. As an added bonus, the soya plant itself is also good for the environment, as it adds nutrients to the soil that it grows in, does not require pesticides to be grown and is therefore entirely sustainable.

Alpaca

Another yarn growing in popularity with knitters and yarn manufacturers. The alpaca (or llama) is commonly found in Peru and the growing popularity is well justified. It is said to be the warmest fibre on earth and indeed it is indescribably soft and fluffy when worked up. A lightweight DK ply, it gives a luxurious finish which is great for a wide variety of projects. The fluffy fibres, contrary to what one might think, do not spark allergies because it is often the lanolin content which triggers the allergy and alpaca is actually lanolin and dander free, giving it naturally hypo-allergenic properties. All this makes it perfect for baby's skin and anyone who can't wear pure wool next to their skin.

Cotton

The cotton industry has gotten bad press over it's use of artificial pesticides and fertilizers and heavy chemical processing. However, cotton is a popular choice for crochet. It shows texture wonderfully and gives a classic finish. So, I have chosen a good quality cotton yarn which has organic status. It is wonderfully soft to work with and a good substitute for the more commercially grown alternatives. The dying process uses natural colours which produce a delicious mix of lovely soft, pastel shades which are ideal for babies, toddlers and grown-ups too.

Wool

Organic wool is produced without the use of organo-phosphate dips and the sheep must be free to roam and have rotational grazing. After these happy sheep have been shorn, the wool is hand sorted and 'finished' without acids, shrink-proofing, bleaches or moth-proofing. Only vegetable-based soaps are used within the washing process so the finished skein is as pure and natural as possible. Wool comes in different plys and is a great choice for many crochet projects. It is also a perfect choice for felting.

Babies
(0-12 months)

alpaca heart
blanket
pattern page 42

alpaca heart blanket
pattern page 42

cotton Archie
bear & blankie
pattern page 46

cotton Archie
bear & blankie
pattern page 46

cotton Archie bear
romper suit pattern page 50

corn fibre dress,
leggings & scarf
pattern page 56

alpaca sleeping bag & hat
pattern page 60

wool hooded cardigan
pattern page 64

cotton
matinée
jacket
pattern
page 68

wool minstrel hat

pattern page 72

wool minstrel boots

pattern page 74

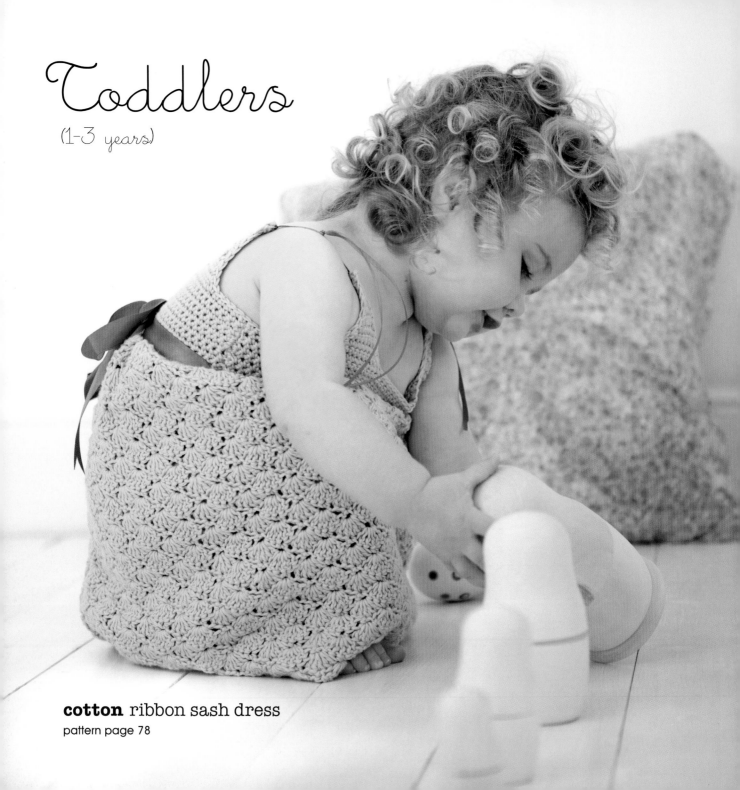

Toddlers
(1-3 years)

cotton ribbon sash dress

pattern page 78

cotton tank top & beanie
pattern page 82

wool
swing
jacket
pattern page 86

alpaca ribbon shrug

pattern page 90

wool
single-breasted
jacket
pattern page 94

wool
tweed
zipped
cardigan
pattern page 98

wool star sweater
pattern page 102

cotton granny square jacket
pattern page 106

Accessories

soya & cotton nappy pants

pattern page 112

soya nursing cushion cover
pattern page 116

cotton cot mobile
pattern page 118

PART ONE

Babies

(0–12 months)

alpaca heart blanket

This soft and cuddly alpaca blanket would make the perfect gift for a newborn baby. It has been worked in soft greys and blues but you could also use baby pink alongside the creams and charcoal if you would prefer.

Sizes

Each square 6 x 6in (15 x 15cm)
Finished blanket 25 x 25in (63.5 x 63.5cm)

Materials

Artesano Inca Cloud 100% pure superfine alpaca (121m/131yd per 50g ball)
2 x 50g balls Ice Blue
2 x 50g balls Cream
2 x 50g balls Charcoal
3.5mm (USE/4) crochet hook
Tapestry needle

Tension

19 sts x 13 rows over 4in (10cm) in half treble stitch

Half treble stitch

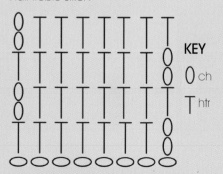

KEY
0 ch
T htr

Blanket

HEART SQUARE

Using 3.5mm (USE/4) hook, make 31ch.

Foundation row (RS) 1htr into 3rd chain from hook, 1htr into each ch, turn. 29 sts.

Row 1 2ch, 1htr into each st, turn.

Rep this st patt throughout the square, working through each row of the heart chart on page 44 and incorporating the colour changes.

COLOUR COMBINATIONS

(make 4 of each)

Cream background and Blue heart

Charcoal background and Blue heart

Blue background and Cream heart

Blue background and Charcoal heart

MAKING UP

Darn in all loose yarn ends. Pin and then block each square into shape. Using contrast yarn, work blanket stitch around each heart. Using the chart on page 45 as a guide, position each square in place and join seams with dc in Charcoal.

EDGING

Using 3.5mm (USE/4) hook and Cream, join yarn anywhere on edge of blanket with a ss.

Foundation row 1ch, work a row of dc evenly around blanket edge, working 3dc into each of the 4 corners and joining the rnd with a ss to first ch.

Row 2 1ch, 1dc into each dc, working 3dc into each of the 4 corners and joining the rnd with a ss to 1st ch. Change to Ice Blue and work as for row 2.

Change to Charcoal and work a final row of crab stitch (see box below). Fasten off.

Crab stitch edging

This is effectively 'reverse' double crochet, worked in the opposite direction to normal (left to right rather than right to left) and it makes a neat 'corded' edging.

* Keeping RS facing, push hook through the top of the next st on the right. Yrh, and pull through (making a total of two loops on the hook). Yrh again, and pull through both loops (1 crab st worked). Rep from * to end.

Heart chart 29 sts x 20 rows

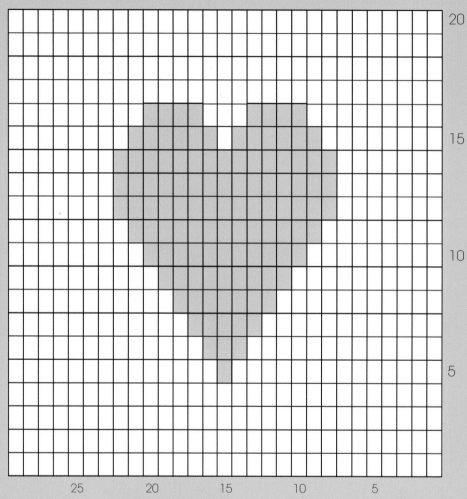

KEY

☐ Main colour
☐ Contrast colour

Each block = 1 st and 1 row

Layout of the blanket

cotton Archie bear & blankie

This traditional teddy bear is so soft and cute; your baby will love to snuggle up to him. He comes with his own heart comfort blankie and would make a great gift paired with the heart baby blanket project on page 42.

Materials

ARCHIE BEAR
Sirdar Sublime Organic Cotton DK
(110m/120yd per 50g ball)
2 x 50g balls 97 Nutmeg (MC)
1 x 50g ball 93 Maize (CC)
Blue ribbon
Cornish organic toy stuffing
Black or brown embroidery thread
for embroidering bear features
3.5mm (USE/4) crochet hook
Row counter

ARCHIE'S BLANKIE
One square from the heart blanket project (Cream background and blue heart, see page 43), blue ribbon and a length of Artesano Inca Cloud yarn in Charcoal for the border.

Tension

Not critical

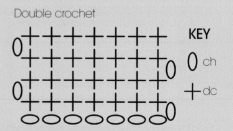

Double crochet

KEY

0 ch

+ dc

Archie bear

LEGS (make 2 alike)

Using 3.5mm (USE/4) hook and CC, make 2 ch.

Foundation rnd Work 6dc into 2nd ch from hook, join to 1st dc with ss to close rnd. 6 sts.

Rnd 1 1ch (counts as 1dc), 1dc into st at base of ch, (2dc in next st) 5 times, ss to 1ch at beg of rnd. 12 sts.

Rnd 2 1ch (counts as 1dc), 1dc into st at base of ch, 1dc in next st, (2dc in next st, 1dc into foll st) 5 times, ss to 1ch at beg of rnd. 18 sts. *

Rnd 3 1ch (counts as 1dc), 1dc into st at base of ch, 1dc in each of next 2 sts, (2dc in next st, 1dc in each of foll 2 sts) 5 times, sl st to 1ch at beg of rnd. 24 sts. **

Change to MC

Rnd 4 1ch (counts as 1dc), 1dc into each st to end, ss to top of 1ch at beg of rnd.

Rnds 5–8 As rnd 4.

Rnd 9 1ch (counts as 1dc), 1dc into each of next 3 sts, dc2tog, (1dc in each of next 4 sts, dc2tog) 3times, ss to 1ch at beg of rnd. 20 sts.

Rep rnd 4 until leg measures 5in (13cm).

Next rnd 1ch (counts as 1dc), 1dc into each of next 2 sts, dc2tog, (1dc in each of next 3 sts, dc2tog) 3 times, ss to 1ch at beg of rnd. 16 sts.

Next rnd As rnd 4.

Next rnd 1ch (counts as 1dc), 1dc into next st, dc2tog, (1dc in each of next 2 sts, dc2tog) 3 times, ss to 1ch at beg of rnd. 12 sts.

Next rnd As rnd 4.

Stuff leg firmly with toy stuffing before you close the top any further.

Next rnd (Dc2tog) to end. 6 sts.

Break off yarn, leaving a long tail. Thread yarn tail onto tapestry needle. Run a line of gathering stitches around top of leg and pull opening firmly shut. Fasten off.

ARMS (make 2 alike)

Using 3.5mm (USE/4) hook and CC, work as for legs to *. 18 sts.

Change to MC.

Work as rnd 4 for legs until arm measures 5in (13cm).

Next rnd 1ch (counts as 1dc), 1dc into each of next 3 sts, dc2tog, (1dc in each of next 4 sts, dc2tog) twice, ss to 1ch at beg of rnd. 15 sts.

Next rnd As rnd 4.

Next rnd 1ch (counts as 1dc), dc2tog (1dc into next st, dc2tog) 4 times, ss to 1ch at beg of rnd. 10 sts.

Next rnd As rnd 4.

Stuff arm firmly with toy stuffing before you close the opening any further.

Next rnd (Dc2tog) to end. 5 sts.

Break off yarn, leaving a long tail. Finish arm top as for leg.

MUZZLE

Using 3.5mm (USE/4) hook and CC, work as for legs to **. 24 sts.

Rnd 4 1ch (counts as 1dc), 1dc into st at base of chain, 1dc in each of next 5 sts (2dc in next st, 1dc in each of 5 foll sts) 3 times, ss to 1ch at beg of rnd. 28 sts.

Rnd 5-8 As rnd 4 of legs.
Break off yarn, leaving a long tail.

HEAD

Using 3.5mm (USE/4) hook and MC, make 2 ch.

Foundation rnd Work 6dc into 2nd ch from hook, join to 1st dc with ss to close rnd. 6 sts.

Rnd 1 1ch (counts as 1dc), 1dc into st at base of ch, (2dc in next st) 5 times, ss to 1ch at beg of rnd. 12 sts.

Rnd 2 and all even rnds 1ch (counts as 1dc), 1dc into each st to end, ss to 1ch at beg of rnd.

Rnd 3 1ch (counts as 1dc), 1dc into st at base of ch, 1 dc into next st, (2dc into next st, 1dc into next dc) 5 times, ss to 1ch at beg of rnd. 18 sts.

Rnd 5 1ch (counts as 1dc), 1dc into st at base of ch, 1dc into each of next 2 sts, (2dc into next st, 1dc into each of next 2 sts) 5 times, ss to 1ch at beg of rnd. 24 sts.

Rnd 7 1ch (counts as 1dc), 1dc into st at base of ch, 1dc into each of next 3 sts, (2dc into next st, 1dc into each of next 3 sts) 5 times; ss to 1ch at beg of rnd. 30 sts.

Rnd 9 1ch (counts as 1dc), 1dc into st at base of ch, 1dc into each of next 4 sts, (2dc into next st, 1dc into each of next 4 sts) 5 times, ss to 1ch at beg of rnd. 36 sts.

Rnd 11 1ch (counts as 1dc), 1dc into st at base of ch, 1dc into each of next 5 sts, (2dc into next st, 1dc into each of next 5 sts) 5 times, ss to 1ch at beg of rnd. 42 sts. ***

Work straight (as for rnd 2) for a further 2.5in (6.5cm).

**** Reset row counter to 0, and now work decs in rev as folls:

Rnd 1 1ch (does not count as first st), (dc2tog, 1dc into each of next 5 sts) 6 times, ss to 1st dc2tog. 36sts.

Rnd 2 and all foll even rnds Work straight (as rnd 2).

Rnd 3 1ch (does not count as first st) (dc2tog, 1dc into each of next 4 sts) 6 times, ss to 1st dc2tog. 30 sts.

Rnd 5 1ch (does not count as first st) (dc2tog, 1dc into each of next 3 sts) 6 times, ss to 1st dc2tog. 24 sts.

Rnd 7 1ch (does not count as first st) (dc2tog, 1dc into each of next 2 sts) 6 times, ss to 1st dc2tog. 18 sts.

Rnd 9 1ch (does not count as first st) (dc2tog, 1dc into next st) 6 times, ss to 1st dc2tog. 12 sts.

Stuff head firmly with toy stuffing before closing opening any further. Finish as for legs and arms.

EARS (make 2 pieces in MC and 2 in CC)

Using 3.5mm (USE/4) hook, make a loop, 6dc into loop, don't join. Pull loop tight to close hole. Turn.

Row 1 1ch (counts as 1dc), 1dc into st at base of ch, 2dc into each of next 5 ch, turn. 12 sts.

Row 2 1ch (counts as 1dc), 1dc into st at base of ch, 1dc into next st (2dc into next st, 1dc into foll st) 5 times, turn. 18 sts.

Row 3 1ch, 1dc into each st to end. Break off yarn.

Place CC ear on top of MC ear. Use MC to join both ears by working a row of dc through both sets of sts around curved edge of semi-circle. Fasten off.

BODY

Work as for head until ***.
Work straight (as for rnd 2 of head) for a further 4in (10cm).
Now work again as for head, from ****
to end.

MAKING UP

Fill the muzzle with stuffing and pin in position onto the head (refer to photos). Stitch neatly into place with firm stitches. Position the ears at the sides of the head and sew firmly in place. Take a length of embroidery thread and using photo for reference; embroider the nose in satin stitch, the mouth in back stitch and both eyes in satin stitch. Position head onto body and stitch firmly in place. Position arms and legs and sew these in place very firmly. Snip a length of blue ribbon and tie a bow around Archie's neck.

Comfort blankie

Make one of the squares from the heart blanket project (see page 43). I've used Cream and Ice Blue, but you can choose any colours that suit. Work a round of double crochet around the edge of the square in Charcoal to finish (see page 139) and sew a loop of blue ribbon firmly to one corner long enough to fit over his paw.

gethooked

As with all toys for young children, remember to sew everything firmly in place and check the seams every so often in case Archie sheds a few stitches from over-loving!

cotton Archie bear romper suit

This cute romper is the ideal gift for babies. It has its own matching bear and blankie project to complete the set (see pages 46–49). Again, I have worked the design in blue but it would look equally good in pink or lemon.

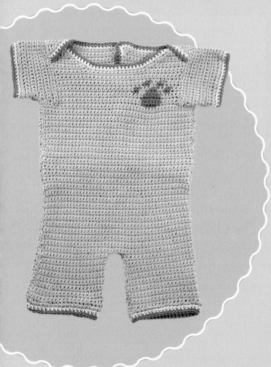

Sizes

	0–6 months	6–12 months
Chest	22in	24in
	56cm	61cm
Finished length	18in	20in
	46cm	51cm
Sleeve	2½in	3in
	6.5cm	8cm
Leg seam	4in	5in
	10cm	13cm

Materials

Sirdar Sublime Organic 100% Cotton DK (110m/120yd per 50g ball)
1[1] x 50g ball in Nutmeg
1[1] x 50g ball in Maize
4[6] x 50g balls in Clay
Oddments of brown/black yarn or thread for embroidery
9[10] buttons (by Stockwell Pottery, see *Suppliers* page 142)
9[10] snap fasteners
4mm (USG/6) crochet hook

Tension

17 sts x 20 rows over 4in (10cm) in double crochet

Double crochet

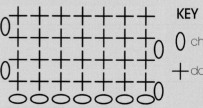

KEY

0 ch

+ dc

Romper suit

FRONT LEGS (make 2 pieces alike)
Using 4mm (USG/6) hook and Clay,
make 22[25]ch.
Foundation row (RS) Miss 1st ch,
dc to end. 21[24] sts.
Row 1 1ch, dc to end.
Rep row 1 until leg measures 3½[4½]in
(9[11.5]cm).
Fasten off.

FRONT BODY

Using 4mm (USG/6) hook and Clay and
with RS facing, rejoin yarn to top edge
of one leg front, 1ch, dc to end, 4ch,
dc across top of other leg front.
46[52] sts.
Next row 1ch, dc to end. **
Rep last row until work (from beg of
legs) measures 13½[15]in (34[38]cm),
ending on a WS row.
Shape armholes
Row 1 With RS facing, ss across 1st 4
sts, 1ch, dc across foll 38[44] sts, do
not work last 4 sts. 38[44] sts.
Row 2 1ch, dc to end.
Next Working even (as set by row 2),
beg working paw print chart (on page
55) as folls:
1ch, dc across 5[8] sts, work 10 sts
from paw print chart, dc across foll
23[26] sts.
Cont as set until chart is complete.

Cont to work even in dc using Clay until
armhole measures 3[3½]in (8[9]cm),
ending on a WS row.
Shape neck (first side)
Row 1 (RS) 1ch, dc across 10[12] sts,
turn.
Row 2 1ch, miss 1 st, dc to end, turn.
9[11] sts.
Row 3 1ch, dc across to last 2dc,
dc2tog, turn. 8[10] sts.
Rep rows 2–3 until 2 sts rem, and
fasten off.
Shape neck (other side)
Row 1 (RS) Miss centre 18[20] sts, join
yarn to 19th[21st] st, 1ch, dc across
10[12] sts to end, turn.
Row 2 1ch, dc across to last 2 sts,
dc2tog, turn. 9[11] sts.
Row 3 1ch, miss 1 st, dc to end, turn.
8[10] sts.
Rep last two rows until 2 sts rem, and
fasten off.

BACK LEGS (make 2 pieces alike)
Work as for front legs.

LOWER BACK

Work as for front body until **.
Rep last row for a further 1in (2.5cm),
ending on a WS row.
Beg Archie bear motif
Row 1 1ch, dc across 13[16] sts, work
20 sts from bear chart (on page 54),
dc across rem 13[16] sts.

gethooked
If you find intarsia crochet
too difficult, you could try using
cross stitch embroidery instead.
Work from the chart as normal
and use one stitch to work one
cross stitch over.

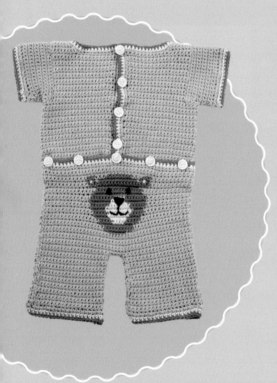

Work through the chart as set. When complete, cont to work even in dc using Clay until until work (from beg of legs) measures 9½[10½]in (24[27]cm).
Fasten off.

RIGHT UPPER BACK

Using 4mm (USG/6) hook and Clay, make 24[27]ch.
Foundation row (RS) Miss 1st ch, dc to end. 23[26] sts.
Row 1 1ch, dc to end.
Rep row 1 until work measures 5[5½]in (13[14]cm), ending on a WS row.
Fasten off.

Shape armhole
Row 1 (RS) Miss first 4 sts, rejoin yarn to next st, 1ch, dc to end. 19[22] sts.
Row 2 1ch, dc to end.
Rep last row until armhole measures 4[4½]in (10[11.5]cm), ending on a WS row.

Shape neck
Row 1 (RS) 1ch, dc across next 8[10] sts, turn.
Row 2 1ch, miss 1 st, dc to end, turn. 7[9] sts.
Row 3 1ch, dc to last 2 sts, dc2tog, turn. 6[8] sts.
Rep last 2 rows until 2 sts rem.
Fasten off.

LEFT UPPER BACK

Work as for right back, rev all shapings.

SLEEVES (make 2 alike)

Using 4mm (USG/6) hook and Clay, make 35[37]ch.
Foundation row (RS) Miss 1st ch, dc to end. 34[36] sts.
Row 1 1ch, 2dc into 1st st, dc to last st, 2dc in last st, turn. 36[38] sts.
Row 2 1ch, dc to end.
Rep rows 1–2 until 38[42] sts.
Then rep row 2 until sleeve measures 2[3]in (5[8]cm).
Fasten off.

MAKING UP

Darn in all loose yarn ends. Press pieces lightly.
Using oddments of brown or black yarn, embroider Archie's nose, mouth and eyes according to the chart.

Front neck edging
Using 4mm (USG/6) hook and Clay, join yarn to top RH point of neck edge.
Row 1 (RS) 1ch, dc evenly along RH neck shaping, across centre sts and then along LH neck shaping, ending at top LH point of neck.
Row 2 (WS) Change to Maize. 1ch, dc to end.
Row 3 (RS) Change to Nutmeg. 1ch, dc to end.
Fasten off.

Right upper back edging

Using 4mm (USG/6) hook and Clay, join yarn to top RH point of neck edge.

Row 1 (RS) 1ch, dc evenly across neck edge, 3dc into corner, then dc evenly down along LH side edge to end.

Row 2 (WS) Change to Maize. 1ch, dc up side edge, 3dc into corner st, then dc across neck to end.

Row 3 (RS) Change to Nutmeg. 1ch, dc across neck, 3dc into corner st, dc down side edge.

Fasten off.

Left upper back edging

Using 4mm (USG/6) hook and Clay, join yarn to bottom RH corner of piece.

Row 1 (RS) 1ch, dc evenly up along side edge, 3dc into corner, then dc evenly across to top LH point of neck edge.

Row 2 (WS) Change to Maize. 1ch, dc across neck edge, 3dc into corner st, then dc down side edge to end.

Row 3 (RS) Change to Nutmeg. 1ch, dc up side edge, 3dc into corner, dc across neck to end.

Fasten off.

Lower back edging

Using 4mm (USG/6) hook and Clay, and with RS facing, join yarn to top RH corner of piece.

Row 1 (RS) 1ch, dc across to end.

Row 2 (WS) Change to Maize. 1ch, dc to end.

Row 3 (RS) Change to Nutmeg. 1ch, dc to end.

Fasten off.

Back fastenings

Lay right and left upper back pieces together, overlapping the edgings where they meet at the centre back. Mark position of 4 snap fasteners along this opening, then sew firmly in place. Next, place lower back piece in position, overlapping the upper piece by 1in (2.5cm). Mark position of 5[6] snap fasteners along this opening, then sew firmly in place. Alternate brown and blue buttons, and sew in place over the snap fasteners on the outside edges. Snap all pieces into position. Place front and back pieces together with WS facing. Position shoulder overlaps and secure with a few stitches. Now flip the work over so that the RS are facing. Pin sleeves into position along armhole edge and sew into place. Next, sew sleeve and side seams. Finally, sew gusset and inside leg seams. Turn RS out.

Leg and arm edgings

With RS facing, using 4mm (USG/6) hook and Clay, join yarn to any st near seam.

Rnd 1 (RS) Dc evenly around leg/arm edge, ending with a ss into 1st dc to join the rnd.

Rnd 2 Change to Maize. 1ch, dc to end of rnd, ss into 1ch to join.

Rnd 3 Change to Nutmeg. 1ch, dc to end of rnd, ss into 1ch to join.

Fasten off. Sew in any loose yarn ends.

Archie bear chart   20 sts x 18 rows

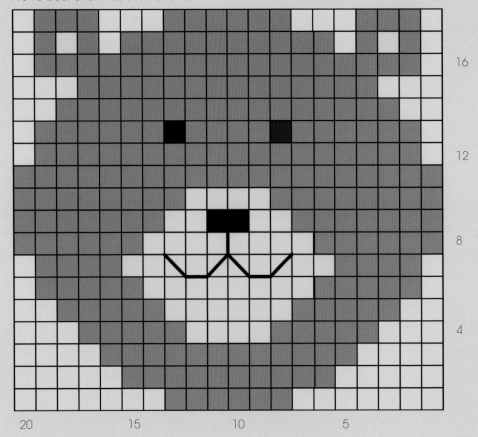

16

12

8

4

20   15   10   5

KEY
☐ Clay
■ Nutmeg
☐ Maize
■ Black (or dark brown)

Each block = 1 st and 1 row
Read RS rows from R to L and WS rows
from L to R

Paw print chart   10 sts x 8 rows

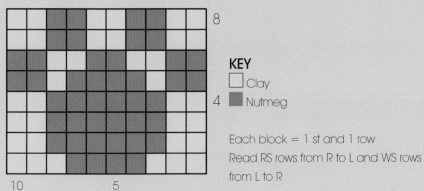

8

4

10   5

KEY

☐ Clay

■ Nutmeg

Each block = 1 st and 1 row

Read RS rows from R to L and WS rows

from L to R

corn fibre dress, leggings & scarf

This pretty dress has leggings and a headscarf to make it a complete outfit that is a perfect summer cover-up for babies. You could just crochet the sundress which would look beautiful with a cute pair of sandals, or worn over jeans or denim shorts.

Sizes

	0–6 months	6–12 months
DRESS		
Finished chest	18in	20in
	46cm	51cm
Length from shoulder	12in	14in
	30.5cm	35.5cm
LEGGINGS		
Leggings waist	20in	22in
	51cm	56cm
Inside leg	4in	5in
	10cm	13cm

Materials

DRESS
SWTC Amaizing 100% Corn Fiber
(130m/142yd per 50g ball)
3[5] x 50g balls in Cream Puff
1 x 50g ball in Princess
2 x pink spot buttons

LEGGINGS
2[3] x 50g balls in Cream Puff
1 x 50g ball in Princess
Elastic for waistband

HEADSCARF
1[1] x 50g balls in Cream Puff
1 x 50g ball in Princess
3.5mm (USE/4) and 4.5mm (US7)
crochet hooks

Tension

18 sts x 16 rows over 4in (10cm) using
4.5mm hook and griddle stitch

Griddle stitch

Foundation row Miss 3ch (counts as 1tr), (1dc into next ch, 1tr into foll ch) to last ch, 1dc into last ch.

Patt rep row 3ch (counts as 1tr), miss 1st st (1dc into next st, 1tr into foll st) to last st, 1dc into top of 3ch.

Sundress

FRONT

Using 4.5m hook (US7) and Cream Puff make 62[72]ch.

Work foundation row in griddle stitch. 60[70] sts.

Rows 1–3 Work patt rep row of griddle stitch patt.

Row 4 (dec row) Patt to last st and turn leaving final st unworked (1 st decreased). 59[69] sts.

Rep row 4 until 40[46] sts rem.

Work even in griddle stitch until work measures 7[8½]in (18[21.5]cm).

Shape armholes

Row 1 Ss across 1st 5 sts, patt to end. 35[41] sts.

Row 2 As row 1. 30[36] sts.

Work even in griddle stitch for 2½[3½]in (6.5[9]cm), ending with a WS row. **

Shape front neck and straps

Work 9[10] sts in patt for 1½in (4cm).

Next row (dec row) Patt to last st, turn leaving rem st unworked
(1 st decreased). 8[9] sts.

Rep last row once[twice]. 7[7] sts.

Work even until strap measures 2in (5cm).

Fasten off.

With RS facing, miss centre 12[16] sts.

Rejoin yarn to next st, patt rem 9[10] sts.

Work second strap to match the first.

gethooked

If you prefer, you can use snap fasteners on the dress straps instead of working a buttonhole.

Griddle stitch

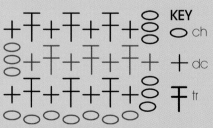

KEY

o ch

+ dc

Ŧ tr

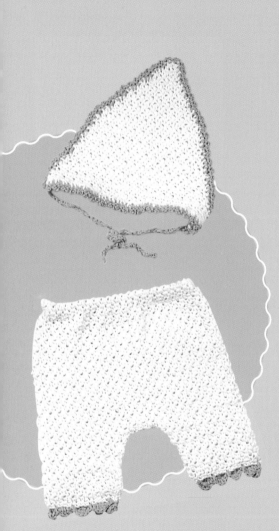

BACK

Work as for front until **

Shape back neck and straps

Work 9[10] sts in patt for 2½in (6.5cm).

Buttonhole row Patt 4 sts, miss 1 st, 1ch, patt 3 sts.

Cont to work even in patt until strap measures 3in (8cm).

Fasten off.

With RS facing, miss centre 12[16] sts. Rejoin yarn to next st, patt rem 9[10] sts. Work second strap to match the first.

MAKING UP

Darn in loose yarn ends. Sew side seams.

Sew buttons to front straps and fasten.

Neck and armhole edging

Using 3.5mm (USE/4) hook and Princess and with RS facing, join yarn to any st along the armpit.

Rnd 1 1ch, work a row of dc evenly along armhole, straps and front and back edges, joining the rnd with a ss to 1ch.

Rnd 2 1ss into next st, (3ch, 1ss into each of next 2 sts) to end, finishing with a ss to 1ch.

Lower trim

Using 3.5mm (USE/4) hook and Cream Puff and with RS facing, join yarn to any stitch near the side seam of skirt.

Rnd 1 1ch, work a row of dc evenly along lower edge of skirt, joining the rnd with a ss to 1ch.

Rnd 2 Change to Princess. 1ch (1dc, 4ch, miss 3dc) to end, joining the rnd with a ss to 1ch.

Rnd 3 1ch, * ss into dc, (1dc, 3tr, 1dc) in ch sp, rep from * to end, ending with ss in last st.

Leggings

FRONT AND BACK

(make 2 pieces alike)

Using 4.5mm (US7) hook and Cream Puff make 48[52]ch.

Work foundation row of griddle stitch. 46[50] sts.

Work in griddle stitch patt for 7½[8½]in (19[21.5]cm).

First leg

Row 1 (RS) Patt over 20[22] sts. *

Row 2 Work even in patt.

Row 3 (dec row) Patt to last st, leave last st unworked (1 st decreased). 19[21] sts.

Rep rows 2–3 once.

Work even on these sts until leg measures 4[5]in (10[13]cm).

Fasten off.

Second leg

Row 1 With RS facing, miss centre 6 sts. Rejoin yarn to next st and patt across rem 20[22] sts.

Work as for 1st leg from * to end.

MAKING UP

Darn in loose yarn ends. Sew side and leg/crotch seams.

Casing

Turn down top (waist) edge 1in (2.5cm) and ss to WS, leaving an opening for elastic. Thread elastic through and adjust to fit waist size. Secure elastic ends with firm stitches. Close opening.

Leg trim

Work as given for lower trim of sundress.

Headscarf (one size)

Using 4.5mm (US7) hook and Cream Puff make 42ch.

Work foundation row of griddle stitch. 40 sts.

Row 1 Work in griddle stitch patt to last st and turn leaving rem st unworked (1 st decreased). 39 sts.

Rep row 1 until 3 sts rem.

Next row Dc3tog.

Fasten off.

Side edgings

Using 3.5mm (USE/4) hook and Princess and with RS facing, join yarn to right corner edge.

Row 1 1ch, work 1 row of dc evenly along first side, working 3dc into point of scarf, then finishing at left corner edge on opposite side.

Row 2 1ss into next st, (3ch, 1ss into each of next 2 sts) to end, finishing with a ss to 1ch.

Front edging and ties

Using 3.5mm (USE/4) hook and Princess make 40ch, dc evenly across front edge of scarf, make another 41ch.

Next row Miss1ch, dc into each of 40 ch, * 1dc into each of next 2dc, (3ch, 1ss into each of next 2 sts) to end of front edge, 1dc into each of 40 ch.

Fasten off.

Darn in loose yarn ends.

alpaca sleeping bag & hat

This snugly hat and sleeping bag are perfect for slipping on over a romper suit.
Worked in classic navy and cream, the star buttons add a colourful finishing touch,
but are purely decorative as I've used poppers to fasten for quick and easy changing.

Sizes

	0–6months
Finished chest	24in (61cm)
Length from shoulder	22in (56cm)
Hat circumference	15in (38cm)

Materials

Artesano Inca Cloud 100%
pure superfine alpaca
(121m/131yd per 50g ball)
3.5mm (USE/4) crochet hook
Tapestry needle
SLEEPING BAG
3 x 50g balls Navy
3 x 50g balls Cream
1 large and 4 medium star buttons in
red (by Stockwell Pottery, see *Suppliers*
page 142)
12 snap fasteners
HAT
1 x 50g ball Navy
1 x 50g ball Cream
1 medium red star button

Tension

19 sts x 13 rows over 4in (10cm) using
3.5mm hook in half treble stitch

Stripe pattern

2 rows Cream, 2 rows Navy

Double crochet for edging

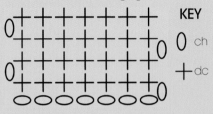

KEY

O ch

+ dc

Half treble stitch

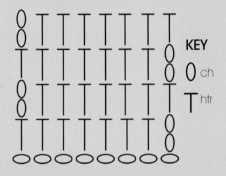

KEY

O ch

T htr

Hat

Using 3.5mm (USE/4) hook and Cream, make 72ch.

Foundation row Miss 3 ch, 1htr into each ch st to end. 70 sts.

Next row 2 ch, 1htr into each st to end. Rep last row, working even in stripe patt, until work measures 6in (15cm). Fasten off.

Darn in loose yarn ends. Press lightly. Sew up rear seam of hat. Sew top seam of hat.

EDGING

Foundation rnd Using Navy and with RS facing, join yarn to lower edge of hat, 1ch, work a rnd of dc evenly around edge, ss to 1ch to join rnd.

Rows 1–5 1ch, 1dc into each st, ss to 1ch to join rnd.

Fasten off and darn in yarn ends. Fold hat tips together and sew. Place button on join and sew firmly in place.

gethooked

Although I've worked this project in stripes, you could make things easier by just working one solid colour and perhaps using a contrast colour for the edging.

Sleeping bag

BACK

Using 3.5mm (USE/4) hook and Cream, make 62ch.

Foundation row (RS) Miss 3 ch, 1htr into each ch st to end. 60 sts.

Next row 2 ch, 1htr into each st to end. Rep last row, working even in stripe patt, until work measures 16in (41cm). Break off yarn.

Shape armholes

Miss 1st 5 sts, rejoin yarn to next st, make 2 ch, 1htr into each of next 50 sts, turn. 50 sts.

Keeping to stripe patt, work even for a further 5in (13cm).

Fasten off.

FRONT

There is a lot of shaping in the front flaps. Remember to keep to the stripe patt (2 rows Cream, 2 rows Navy) throughout.

Left flap

Using 3.5mm (USE/4) hook and Cream, make 12ch.

Foundation row (RS) Miss 3 ch, 1htr into each ch st to end. 10 sts.

Rows 1–3 2ch, 1htr into each st to end.

Row 4 (inc row) 2ch, htr across until last st, 2htr into last st. 11 sts.

Row 5 (inc row) 2ch, 2htr into first st, htr to end. 12 sts.

Rep rows 4–5 until there are 50 sts.

** Next (dec row) 2ch, htr across until last 2 sts, htr2tog. 49 sts.

Next (dec row) 2ch, miss 1st st, htr to end. 48 sts.

Still keeping to stripe patt, rep these 2 dec rows until there are 40 sts.

Break off yarn.

Shape armhole

Miss 1st 5 sts. Rejoin yarn to next st, htr across until last 2 sts, htr2tog. 34 sts.

Cont to dec 1 st at neck edge as set, until 27 sts rem.

Shape neck

Next 2ch, 1htr into each of next 22 sts. 22 sts.

Cont to dec 1 st at neck edge as set until 18 sts rem.

Work even in stripe patt until front measures same as back.

Fasten off.

Right flap

Using 3.5mm hook and Cream make 62ch.

Foundation row (RS) Miss 3 ch, 1htr into each ch st to end. 60 sts.

Rows 1–3 2ch, 1htr into each st to end, remembering to work in stripe patt.

Work even until back flap measures 10 rows less than front flap at widest point.

Next (dec row) 2ch, htr across to last 2 sts, htr2tog. 59 sts.

Next (dec row) 2ch, miss 1st st, htr to end. 58 sts.

Still keeping to stripe patt, rep these 2 dec rows until 50 sts rem.

Work as for left flap from ** to end, reversing all shapings.
Fasten off.

MAKING UP

Darn in all loose yarn ends and press lightly.
Join shoulder and side seams.

Front border

With RS facing, using 3.5mm (USE/4) hook and Navy, join yarn to bottom corner of right front with a ss, 1ch, work a row of dc evenly up right front, across back of neck and down left front, working 3dc into front corners and points, turn.

Rows 1–2 1ch, 1dc into each st, working 3dc into front corners and points, turn.
Fasten off.

Lower button border

Using 3.5mm hook and Navy and with RS facing, join yarn to corner of lower edge, 1ch, work a row of dc evenly across bottom edge of left flap, back and right flap, turn.

Rows 1–6 1ch, 1dc into each st, turn.
Fasten off.

Armhole edging

Using 3.5mm (USE/4) hook and Navy and with RS facing, join yarn to armhole edge, 1ch, work a round of dc evenly around armhole, ending with a ss to 1ch to join.

Rows 1–2 1ch, 1dc into each st, ending with a ss to 1ch to join.
Fasten off.
Rep for 2nd armhole.

Darn in any rem yarn ends. Fold flaps into place. Position 8 snap fasteners evenly along the join between right and left front flaps, from neck to lower border. Sew firmly in place. Position 4 snap fasteners evenly between back and front, along lower button border. Sew firmly in place. Sew large red star button to the front flap at point. Sew 4 medium red star buttons along button border directly over the place where the snap fasteners are positioned.

wool hooded cardigan

This comfy and warm hooded cardigan is ideal for chilly winter outings to the park. Just throw on over baby jeans and a t-shirt for a fun, warm and snugly trip outside.

Sizes

	0–6 months	6–12 months	12–18 months
Finished chest	21in	24in	26in
	53.5cm	61cm	66cm
Length from shoulder	10½in	11in	12in
	27cm	28cm	30.5cm
Sleeve	7in	8in	9in
	18cm	20.5cm	23cm

Materials

Sirdar Eco wool DK 100% un-dyed
Virgin Wool (100m/109yd per 50g ball)
2[3:3] x 50g balls 203 Earth
2[3:3] x 50g balls 201 Natural
2[3:3] x 50g balls 200 Ecru
4.5mm (US7) crochet hook
6 wooden duffle buttons

Tension

16 sts x 12 rows over 4in (10cm)
in long wave stitch pattern

SPECIAL ABBREVIATION

Grp group (worked over 14 sts)
1dc into next st, (1htr into next st) twice, (1tr into next st) twice, (1dtr into next st) 3 times, (1tr into next st) twice, (1htr into next st) twice, (1dc into next st) twice.

RevGrp reverse group (worked over 14 sts)
1dtr into next st, (1tr into next st) twice, (1htr into next st) twice, (1dc into next st) 3 times, (1htr into next st) twice, (1tr into next st) twice, (1dtr into next st) twice.

Stripe pattern

Work (2 rows in Earth, 2 rows in Natural and 2 rows in Ecru), rep for stripe pattern.

Long wave pattern

Row 1 (RS) Miss 2ch (count as 1dc), (1Grp over next 14ch) to end.

Row 2 1ch (count as 1dc), miss 1st st, 1dc into next and each st to end, working last dc into top of turning ch.

Row 3 4ch (counts as 1dtr), miss 1st st, (1RevGrp over next 14 sts) to end.

Row 4 As row 2.

Row 5 1ch (counts as 1dc), miss 1st st, (1Grp over next 14 sts) to end, working last dc in turning ch.

Row 6 As row 2.

Rep rows 3–6 for patt.

Double crochet for edging and toggles

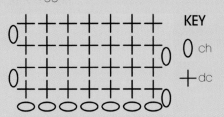

KEY

O ch

+ dc

Long wave stitch

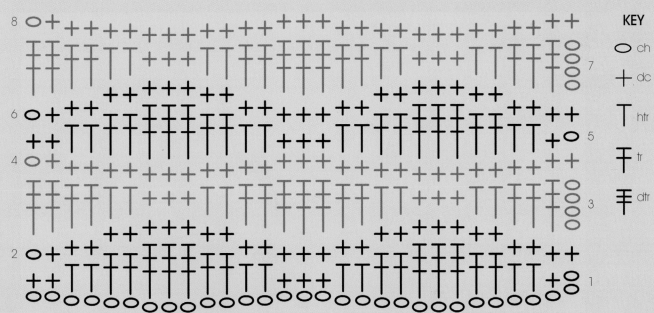

KEY

O ch

+ dc

T htr

T̄ tr

T̄̄ dtr

Cardigan

BODY

Using 4.5mm (US7) hook and Earth, make 86[100:114]ch.

Work rows 1–2 in long wave st patt. 85[99:113] sts.

Switch to Natural and work patt rows 3–4. Switch to Ecru and work patt rows 5–6.

Cont to work even in long wave st patt, changing colours every 2 rows for stripe patt, until body measures 6[6:6½]in (15[15:16.5]cm) ending with RS facing for next row.

Divide for right front

Patt 21[24:28] sts, turn.

Keeping to patt, work even for a further 2½[3:3½]in (6.5[8:9]cm), ending with a WS row.

Shape neck

Ss across 1st 6 sts of next row, patt to end, turn. 15[18:22] sts.

Cont to work in patt, dec 1 st at neck edge over the next 5[6:6] rows. 10[12:16] sts.

Work even in patt until armhole measures 4½[5:5½]in (11.5[13:14]cm) ending with a WS row. Fasten off.

Back

With RS facing, miss next st.

Rejoin yarn with a ss to foll st. Patt 41[49:55] sts, turn.

Work even in patt on these sts until back measures the same as right front, ending on a WS row. Fasten off.

Left front

With RS facing, miss next st, rejoin yarn and patt across rem 21[24:28] sts. Work as for right front, rev shapings.

HOOD

Join shoulder seams.

With WS facing and using 4.5mm (US7) hook, rejoin Earth yarn with ss to left front neck edge.

Work 12dc evenly up front neck, 1dc into next 4[8:11] sts along back of neck, 2dc into each of next 12[8:5] sts, 1dc into rem 5[9:12] sts, Work 12dc evenly down right front neck. 57[57:57] sts.

Work row 1 of long wave st patt. 56[56:56] sts.

Cont to work in long wave and stripe patts as for body, until hood measures 7[7½:8]in (18[19:20.5]cm).

Fold hood in half with RS facing together. Join seam by working dc through both sets of sts. Fasten off.

SLEEVES (make 2 alike)

Using 4.5mm (US7) hook and Earth, make 30ch.

Work row 1 of long wave st patt. 29 sts.

Keeping to long wave and stripe patts, inc 1 st at each end of every foll 6th[4th:4th] row until there are 36[40:44] sts. Work even in patts until sleeve measures 7[8:9]in (18[20.5:23]cm). Fasten off.

MAKING UP

Darn loose yarn ends. Press pieces under a damp cloth. Pin and sew sleeve seams. Sew sleeves into armholes. Make a pompom in Earth and sew firmly to point of hood.

Body edging

With RS facing and using 4.5mm (US7) hook and Earth, attach yarn to lower edge of cardigan below one armhole, 1ch (does not count as st) work 1 rnd of dc evenly around entire hem, front openings and hood edgings, working 3dc into hem corners, ending with ss to 1ch.
Fasten off.

Cuff edgings

With RS facing, using 4.5mm hook and Earth, attach yarn to sleeve edge, 1ch (does not count as st), work 1 round of dc evenly around lower edge, ending with ss into 1ch.
Fasten off.

Duffle loops (make 3 alike)

With 4.5mm (US7) hook and Earth, make 6ch, ss to 6th ch from hook, 12 ch, ss to 6th ch from hook, do not turn.

Next 1ch, miss ch used for last ss, 1dc into next 6ch, 1dc into each of 1st 2 ch of starting loop, 2dc into each of next 2 ch, 1 dc into each of last 2 ch of starting loop, work 1dc into each of next 6 sts (working back along other side of joining loop), 1dc into 1st 2 ch

of 2nd loop, 2dc into each of next 2 ch, 1dc into last 2 ch of 2nd loop, ss to 1st dc. Fasten off.

Position duffle loops onto the front of cardigan. Sew right (for girl) or left (for boy) loop firmly in place. Sew duffle button on top of loop. Rep for the rest of duffle loops. Line up corresponding buttons on opposite side of cardigan and sew in place. Fasten toggle.

gethooked

This pattern has a fairly complicated repeat. The stitch diagram will be your best friend! If you lose your way mid-row, place your work next to the diagram and you will be able to match it to the shape quite easily.

cotton matinée jacket

This classic design is a must for every baby girl's wardrobe. I've reworked it using Quebracho Bark and Chocolate but it would work equally well in more traditional pinks, lemons or even minty green.

Sizes

	0–3 months	3–6 months	6–12months
Finished chest	18in	20in	22in
	46cm	51cm	56cm
Length from shoulder	10in	11cm	12in
	25.5cm	28cm	30.5cm
Sleeve	5½in	6½in	7½in
	14cm	16.5cm	19cm

Materials

Rowan Purelife 100% organic cotton
(120m/130yd per 50g ball)
3[3:4] x 50g balls 987 Quebracho Bark
3.5mm (USE/4) crochet hook
Length of chocolate velvet ribbon
3 x cream pearl buttons

Tension

15 sts x 10 rows over 4in (10cm)
in forget-me-not stitch
17 sts x 20 rows over 4in (10cm)
in double crochet stitch

Forget-me-not stitch pattern

See also forget-me-not stitch diagram (below)

Foundation row (1tr, 2ch, 1dc) in 3rd ch st * miss 2 ch, (2tr, 2ch, 1dc) in next ch, rep from * to end.

Row 1 2ch, (1tr, 2ch, 1dc) in 2ch sp, * (2tr, 2ch, 1dc) in 2ch sp, rep from * to end.
Rep row 1 for patt.

Forget-me-not stitch for skirt of jacket

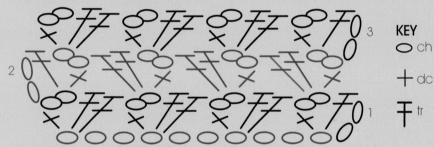

KEY

⬯ ch

✛ dc

⊤ tr

Double crochet for bodice of jacket

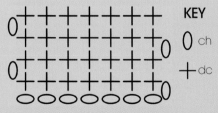

KEY

0 ch

+ dc

Matinée jacket

LOWER SKIRT

Using 3.5mm (USE/4) hook, make 81[90:99]ch.

Work in forget-me-not st patt until skirt measures 5½[6:6½]in (14[15:16.5]cm). Fasten off.

JACKET BODY

Using 3.5mm (USE/4) hook, make 79[91:95]ch.

Foundation row (RS) Miss 1st ch, 1dc into each ch st to end. 78[90:94] sts.

Row 1 (eyelet row) 2ch, 1 tr into each st.

Rows 2–3 1ch, 1dc into each st.

Divide for right front (beg armhole)

Row 5 (RS) 1ch, dc across 19[22:23] sts.

Work even in dc on these sts only for a further 2[2.5:3]in (5[6.5:8]cm), ending with WS facing for next row.

Neck shaping

Row 1 1ch, dc across 18[21:22] sts, miss last st. 18[21:22] sts

Row 2 1ch, miss 1st st, dc to end. 17[20:21]dc.

Rep rows 1–2 until 10[13:14] sts rem. Work even until armhole measures 4[4.5:5]in (10[11.5:13]cm). Fasten off.

Back

With RS facing, miss 1dc, rejoin yarn to next dc, 1ch, dc across 38[44:46] sts. Next row 1ch, dc to end.

Work even on these 38[44:46] sts until back measures the same as right front. Fasten off.

Left front

With RS facing, miss 1dc, rejoin yarn to next st, 1ch, dc to end. 19[22:23] sts. Work as for right front, rev all shapings.

SLEEVES (make 2 alike)

Using 3.5mm (USE/4) hook, make 25[27:29]ch.

Foundation row Miss 1st ch, 1dc into each ch st to end. 24[26:28]dc.

Row 1 1ch, dc to end.

Row 2 (inc row) 1ch, 2dc into 1st st, dc to last st, 2dc into last st. 26[28:30] sts. Cont in dc as set, inc on every foll 4th row until there are 34[38:42] sts. Work even until sleeve measures 5½[6½:7½]in (14[16.5:19]cm). Fasten off.

MAKING UP

Darn in loose yarn ends and press according to ball band instructions. Pin and sew sleeve seams. Sew sleeves into armholes. Run a line of gathering stitches along top of skirt, adjust to fit lower body edge. Pin and sew neatly to the jacket body.

Cuff edging

With RS facing, rejoin yarn to lower edge of sleeve, 1ch, dc evenly around edge, ss into 1ch to join. Next rnd 1ch, dc to end, ss to 1ch to join.

Rep last rnd once. Fasten off.

Jacket edging

With RS facing and using 3.5mm (USE/4) hook, join yarn to lower edge of jacket body on right front (at the point where the skirt is attached).

Foundation row 1ch, work a row of dc evenly around the top half of the jacket i.e. right front edge, back of neck and left front edge, ending at the point where the skirt is attached and working 3dc into the 2 front corners (at front centre neck).

Buttonhole row 1ch, dc along left front edge, 3dc into corner st, dc along neck edge, 3dc into corner st, 1dc into next 3dc, (1ch and miss next st to form buttonhole, 1dc into each of next 4dc) twice, (1ch and miss next st to form last buttonhole), dc to end.

Next row 1ch, 1dc into every dc and ch sp to end. Fasten off.

Darn in loose yarn ends.

Position buttons and sew in place. Thread velvet ribbon through the eyelet row and tie into a bow.

get hooked

The beauty of lacy patterns like this forget-me-not stitch is that they make their own scallops so you've no need to add a border to finish the edge.

wool minstrel hat & boots

This quirky hat and bootee set is sure to cheer your little one even on the darkest of winter days. The bright triangles and colourful crochet pompoms are certain to bring a smile to baby and grown-ups alike.

Sizes

	6–12 months
Head circumference	16in (41cm)
Hat height	7in (18cm)
Foot length	4½in (11.5cm)

Materials

Cornish Organic Wool DK
(230m/251yd per 100g skein)
1 x 100g skein St Hilary (Amber)
1 x 100g skein St Ives (Blue)
1 x 100g skein St Blazey (Pink)
1 x 100g skein St Eval (Green)
1 x 100g skein St Mawes (Navy)
Cornish organic wool toy stuffing
4mm (USG/6) crochet hook
Tapestry needle

Tension

17 sts x 12 rows over 4in (10cm)
in half treble stitch

Minstrel hat

TRIANGLES (make 2 Navy, 1 Amber and 1 Pink)

Using 4mm (USG/6) hook, make 34ch.

Foundation row (RS) Miss 3 ch, 1 htr in each ch to end. 32 sts.

Row 1 2ch, miss 1st st, 1htr into each st until last 2 sts, htr2tog. 30 sts.

Rep row 1 until 2 sts rem.

Next row Htr2tog.

Fasten off.

MAKING UP

Press pieces and darn in loose yarn ends. Lay flat as shown in diagram. Join seam lines (marked in green) with a row of dc worked in Navy (see diagram on page 75). Then fold hat as shown and join final seam (marked in red) as before, with a row of dc worked in Navy. Join top seam (marked in orange) with a row of dc worked in Navy.

Hat edging

Using 4mm (USG/6) hook, join Navy yarn to lower edge of hat with a ss.

Foundation rnd 1ch, work a row of dc evenly around edge of hat, join to 1st ch with a ss to join rnd.

Rnds 1–4 1ch, dc around to end, ss to 1st ch to join rnd.

Fasten off. Darn in loose yarn ends and press.

Pompoms (make 2 Navy, 1 Blue, 1 Amber, 1 Pink and 1 Green)

Using 4mm (USG/6) hook, make 2ch.

Foundation rnd Work 6dc into 2nd ch from hook, ss to 1st dc to join rnd. 6 sts.

Rnd 1 1ch, 2dc into each st, ss to 1st ch. 12 sts.

Rnds 2 and 3 1ch, dc to end, ss to 1st ch.

Rnd 4 (Dc2tog) to end, ss to 1st dc2tog. 6 sts.

Pull the loop on the hook to make it large and to stop it unravelling. Break off yarn, leaving a long tail. Thread yarn onto tapestry needle. Thread yarn in and out of the 6 rem sts around top of pompom, finishing at base of hook loop. Tuck cast-on tail into heart of pompom, and stuff lightly with toy stuffing. Pull needle with yarn to close ball and secure loop back onto hook. Using yarn tail and hook, make 8ch, then secure pompom to point of

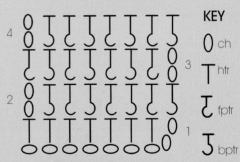

Double crochet for boot uppers and hat band

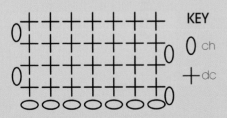

KEY
O ch
+ dc

Half treble for hat

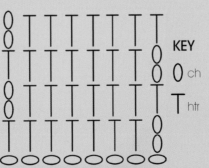

KEY
O ch
T htr

Mock rib for the boot cuffs

KEY
O ch
T htr
⊃ fptr
⊃ bptr

hat with a ss. Darn in loose yarn end so pompom is nice and secure. Try varying the lengths of the pompom chains so they hang from the hat points at random lengths.

Minstrel boots

SOLES (make 2 alike)

Using 4mm (USG/6) hook and Navy, make 10ch.

Foundation rnd Miss 2 ch, 1dc in each of next 8ch, 2ch, swivel work, (1dc into rem 'underneath' strand of next ch st) 8 times.

Rnd 1 (3dc into 2ch space, dc across next 8 sts) twice. 22 sts.

Rnd 2 (2dc into each of the 3 end sts, 1 dc into next 8dc) twice. 28 sts.

Rnd 3 (2dc into each of the 6 end sts, 1dc into next 8dc) twice. 40 sts.

Rnd 4 Dc 12 end sts, dc 8 side sts, dc 12 end sts, dc 4 side sts, tr next 4 side sts.

Rnd 5 (2tr in next dc, 1tr in next dc) 6 times, 2tr in next dc, 1tr in each of next 3dc, 1dc in each of next 3dc, ss in next dc.

Fasten off.

CUFFS (make 2 alike)

Using 4mm (USG/6) hook and Navy, make 30ch.

Mock rib

Note the fptr st appears as a bptr st on the reverse and vice versa, in the same way that a purl st in knitting is a knit st on the reverse side.

Foundation row (RS) Miss 3 ch (counts as a st), 1htr into each ch to end. 28 sts.

Rows 1–5 2ch (counts as 1st st), miss st at base of 2ch, (1fptr around stem of next st, 1bptr around stem of foll st) to end, with final st around 2ch from prev row.

Fasten off.

UPPERS (make 2 alike)

Foundation row Using 4mm (USG/6) hook and with RS of cuff facing, miss first 10 sts, join Pink with a ss and work 1dc into each of the 8 centre sts.

Row 1 (work even) 1ch, 1dc into each st to end.

Row 2 1ch, miss 1st st, 1dc into each st to last 2 sts, dc2tog. 6 sts.

Row 3 As row 1.

Row 4 Dec as for row 2. 4 sts.

Rows 5–7 As row 1.

Row 8 Dec as for row 2. 2 sts.

Row 9–10 As row 1.

Row 11 Dc2tog.

Fasten off.

Insteps

Using 4mm (USG/6) hook and Blue and with RS of cuff facing, join yarn to RH corner of cuff with a ss.

Foundation row 1ch, work 10dc along edge of cuff and 14dc evenly along lower edge of pink upper, turn. 24 sts.

Row 1 1ch, miss 1st dc, 1dc to end, turn. 23 sts.

Row 2 1ch, 1 dc to last 2dc, dc2tog, turn. 22 sts.

Row 3 As row 1. 21 sts.

Row 4 As row 2. 20 sts.

Fasten off.

Second side Using Amber, rejoin yarn to other side of cuff and work as for Blue instep.

Pompoms

Make 2 green pompoms as for hat, omitting the final ch and fastening off with needle and thread on the last rnd.

MAKING UP

Press pieces lightly and darn in loose yarn ends.

Using 4mm (USG/6) hook and Navy, join front toe seams of uppers with a row of dc. Then join rear seam of upper and cuff with a row of dc.

Still using Navy, work a line of relief dc along the triangle seams of the upper to toe point. Fit sole to upper and crochet a row of dc in Navy to join seams. Sew pompom firmly to toe.

Joining the hat

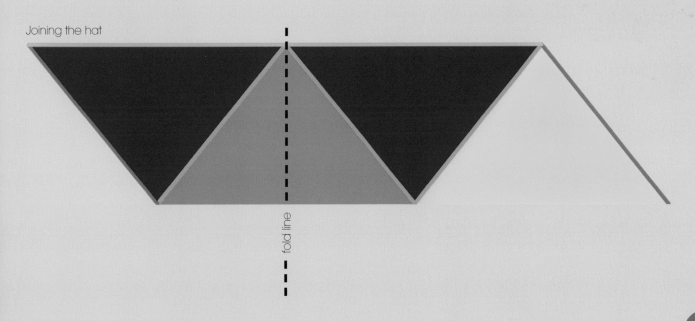

fold line

PART TWO

Toddlers

(1–3 years)

cotton ribbon sash dress

This smart dress is the perfect choice for birthday parties and special occasions. The ribbon ties at waist and shoulder allowing you to adjust the length at knee and chest as your little princess grows and develops.

Sizes

	1–2 years	2–3 years
Finished chest	18in	20in
	46cm	51cm
Finished length	16in	18in
	41cm	46cm
Skirt width (crocheted as one piece)	30in	32in
	76cm	81cm

Materials

Sirdar Sublime Organic DK cotton
(110m/120yd per 50g ball)
4[5] x 50g balls in Peapod
4mm (USG/6) crochet hook
2.2yd (2m) wide green ribbon
1.1yd (1m) narrow green ribbon
3 small buttons

Tension

18 sts x 10 rows over 4in (10cm)
in shell stitch
17 sts x 20 rows over 4in (10cm)
in double crochet

Dress

SKIRT

Using 4mm (USG/6) hook, make 139[145]ch.

Begin working shell stitch patt as folls:

Foundation row (RS) 1dc into 2nd ch from hook, (miss 2ch, 5tr into next ch, miss 2ch, 1dc into next ch) to end. 138[144] sts.

Row 1 3ch (counts as first tr), 2tr into dc at base of 3ch, (miss 2tr, 1dc into next tr, miss 2tr, 5tr into next dc) to last dc, 3tr into last dc.

Row 2 1ch (does not count as st), 1dc into tr at base of 1ch, (miss 2tr, 5tr into next dc, miss 2tr, 1dc into next tr) to end, working last dc into top of 3ch at beg of prev row.

Rep rows 1–2 for patt.

Work even in shell stitch patt until skirt measures 11[12½]in (28[32]cm). Fasten off.

FRONT BODICE

Using 4mm (USG/6) hook, make 39[43]ch.

Foundation row 1dc into 2nd ch from hook, 1dc into each ch to end. 38[42] sts.

Row 1 1ch, 1dc into each st to end.

Work even (as row 1) until front measures 2in (5cm).

Shape armholes

Ss across 1st 4 sts, 1ch, 1dc into next 30[34] sts, turn leaving last 4 sts unworked. 30[34] sts.

Shell stitch

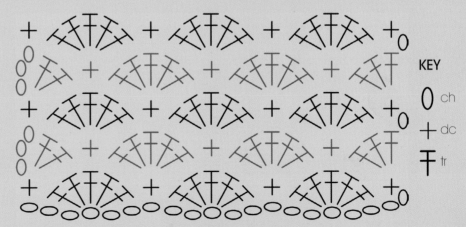

Double crochet

KEY

0 ch

+ dc

KEY

0 ch

+ dc

‡ tr

Next 1ch, miss 1st st, 1dc into each st to last 2 sts, dc2tog. 28[32] sts.

Next 1ch, 1dc into each st to end.

Next 1ch, miss 1st st, 1dc into each st to last 2 sts, dc2tog. 26[30] sts.

Divide for shoulder straps

Next row (RS) 1ch, 1dc into each of next 10 sts, turn leaving rem sts unworked.

Next row 1ch, miss 1st st, 1dc into each st to last 2 sts, dc2tog. 8 sts.

Next row Work even.

Rep these last 2 rows until 2 sts rem. Fasten off.

Second strap

With RS facing, miss centre 6[10] sts, rejoin yarn to next st, 1ch, 1dc into each of next 10 sts.

Work second strap as for first. Fasten off.

BACK RIGHT BODICE

Using 4mm (USG/6) hook, make 20[22]ch.

Foundation row 1dc into 2nd ch from hook, 1dc into each ch to end. 19[21] sts.

Row 1 1ch, 1dc into each st to end. Work even (as row 1) until piece measures 2in (5cm).

Shape armholes and neck

Next row (RS) Ss across 1st 4 sts, 1ch, 1dc into next 12 sts, turn leaving last rem sts unworked (for neck shaping). 10 sts.

Next row 1ch, miss 1st st, 1dc into each st to last 2 sts, dc2tog. 8 sts.

Next row Work even.

Next row 1ch, miss 1st st, 1dc into each st to last 2 sts, dc2tog.

Rep last 2 rows until 2 sts rem. Fasten off.

BACK LEFT BODICE

Work as for back right bodice, rev shapings.

MAKING UP

Darn in loose yarn ends and press pieces lightly. Join the front and back bodices along both side seams. Open out the whole bodice and lay it on a flat surface. Take the skirt and a long length of yarn threaded through a tapestry needle, and run a line of gathering stitches along the width of the skirt on the straight edge (the scalloped edge will be the bottom hem of the dress). Pull up the thread until the skirt fits the width of the bodice. Pin and sew in place. Pin and sew the rear seam of the skirt, leaving 1in (2.5cm) unstitched at the top, for the back opening.

Bodice edging

Using 4mm (USG/6) hook and with RS facing, join to the edge of the bodice at the base of the left opening. Work a row of double crochet up the opening, up the rear left bodice working 3dc at corner, around the armhole, left strap, across front of bodice, around right strap, armhole, and finally down right rear bodice working 3dc into corner and ending at bottom of skirt opening. Fasten off and darn in any loose ends.

Position buttons on the right edge of back bodice and sew in place. Work 3 crochet buttonholes on opposite edge (see page 138). Take the wide ribbon and pin in place across front of dress. Slip stitch in place at upper edge only. This will enable the ribbon to lie flat across the bodice when tying. Leave plenty of length so you can make a large pretty bow at the back of the dress when your little girl is getting dressed.

Finally take the narrow ribbon, snip into 4 equal but generous lengths. Sew in place just inside the top edge of the four straps. Try the dress on your daughter, tie the ribbons in place and snip leaving enough length for a pretty bow and some growing space.

gethooked

If it is chilly, this dress would look lovely with the ribbon shrug (on page 90) over the top. Just make it in matching yarn and ribbon for a complete outfit.

cotton tank top & beanie

This cute and classic combination looks great with classic jeans. I've used soft, organic cotton in fresh spring shades. Team it with an organic t-shirt and a pair of trainers and head for the park.

Sizes

	1–2 years	2–3 years
TANK TOP		
Finished chest	26in	28in
	66cm	71cm
Length	13in	14in
	33cm	36cm
HAT		
Finished circumference	17in	19in
	43cm	48cm

Materials

Sirdar Sublime Organic DK cotton
(110m/120yd per 50g ball)
2[3] x 50g balls in 97 Nutmeg
1 x 50g ball in 98 Rice Pudding
1 x 50g ball in 91 Pea Pod
4mm (USG/6) crochet hook

Tension

16 sts x 15 rows over 4in (10cm)
in half treble stitch

Tank top

BACK

Using 4mm (USG/6) hook and Nutmeg, make 54[58] ch.

Row 1 (RS) Miss 3ch, 1htr in each ch to end. 52[56] sts.

Row 2 (Work even) 2ch, 1htr in each st to end.

Row 3 Change to Rice Pudding and work even (in htr st, as row 1).

Rows 4–5 Work even in Nutmeg.

Rows 6–7 Work even in Rice Pudding.

Rows 8–9 Work even in Nutmeg.

Row 10 Work even in Rice Pudding. Change to Nutmeg and work even until body measures 8½[9]in (22[23]cm), ending with a RS row. Break off yarn.

Shape armholes

(WS) Miss 1st 5 sts of next row, rejoin Nutmeg to next st, 2ch, work 1 htr into each of next 42[46] sts, leaving last 5 sts unworked. 42[46] sts. **

Work even on these sts until armhole measures 4½[5]in (11.5[13]cm).

Shape shoulders

Work 13[14] sts. Break off yarn. Miss next 16[18] sts, rejoin yarn to next st, 2ch, 1htr into each of rem 13[14] sts. Fasten off.

FRONT

Work as for back to **.

Next row (RS) Work even.

Divide for neck

Row 1 (WS) Patt 20[22] sts, turn.

Row 2 2ch, miss 1st htr (to dec 1 st at neck edge), patt to end. 19[21] sts.

Row 3 Patt to last 2 sts, htr2tog (to dec 1 st at neck edge). 18[20] sts.

Rep rows 2–3 until 13[14] sts rem. Work even until front length matches back.

Fasten off.

Second side

With WS facing, miss centre 2 sts, rejoin yarn to next st, 2ch, work 1htr into each st to end. 20[22] sts.

Work 2nd side to match the 1st, rev all shapings.

MAKING UP

Darn in loose yarn ends and press pieces lightly.

Join shoulder seams and side seams.

Lower edging

Using 4mm (USG/6) hook and Peapod and with RS facing, join yarn to lower edge at one of the side seams, 1ch, work a rnd of dc evenly along lower edge, finishing with a ss to 1ch at beg of rnd to join.

Next 1ch, 1dc in each st to end, finishing with a ss to 1ch to join rnd. Fasten off. Darn in loose ends.

Neck edging

Using 4mm (USG/6) hook and Peapod and with RS facing, join yarn at neck edge at one of the shoulder seams, 1ch, work a rnd of dc evenly around neck edge, finishing with a ss to 1ch join rnd.

Next 1ch, 1dc in each st, working dc2tog at front centre neck and finishing with a ss to 1ch to join rnd.

Armholes

Using 4mm (USG/6) hook and Peapod and with RS facing, join yarn to top of one of the side seams, 1ch, work a round of dc evenly around armhole, finishing with a ss to 1ch to at beg of rnd to join.

Fasten off.

Rep for 2nd armhole.

Beanie hat

CROWN

Using 4mm (USG/6) hook and Nutmeg make 4ch. Join with a ss to make a ring.

Rnd 1 2ch (counts as first st), 7htr into centre of ring, ss to top of 2ch. 8 sts.

Rnd 2 2ch (counts as first st), 1htr at base of 2ch, 2htr into each of next 7htr, ss to top of 2ch. 16 sts.

Rnd 3 2ch (counts as first st), 1htr at base of 2ch, 1htr into next st, (2htr into next st, 1htr into next st) 7 times, ss to top of 2ch. 24 sts.

Rnd 4 2ch (counts as first st), 1htr at base of 2ch, 1htr into next 2 sts, (2htr into next st, 1htr into next 2 sts) 7 times, ss to top of 2ch. 32 sts.

Rnd 5 2ch (counts as first st), 1htr at base of 2ch, 1htr into next 3 sts, (2htr into next st, 1htr into next 3 sts) 7 times, ss to top of 2ch. 40 sts.

Rnd 6 2ch (counts as first st), 1htr at base of 2ch, 1htr into next 4 sts, (2htr into next st, 1htr into next 4 sts) 7 times, ss to top of 2ch. 48 sts.

Rnd 7 2ch (counts as first st), 1htr at base of 2ch, 1htr into next 5 sts, (2htr into next st, 1htr into next 5 sts) 7 times, ss to top of 2ch. 56 sts.

Rnd 8 2ch (counts as first st), 1htr at base of 2ch, 1htr into next 6 sts, (2htr into next st, 1htr into next 6 sts) 7 times, ss to top of 2ch. 64 sts.

2nd size only 2ch (counts as first st), 1htr at base of 2ch, 1htr into next 7sts, (2htr into next st, 1 htr into next 7 sts) 7 times, ss to top of 2ch. 72 sts.

Next rnd (both sizes) 2ch (counts as first st), 1htr at base of 2ch, 1htr into every st until end of rnd, ss to top of 2ch. Rep this last rnd until hat measures 5[5½]in (13[14]cm) from the crown.

Change to Rice Pudding and work last rnd once.

Change to Nutmeg and work last rnd twice. Fasten off.

Half treble for hat

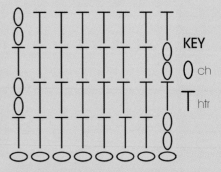

KEY

$\bigcirc$ ch

T htr

MAKING UP

Darn in loose yarn ends and press lightly.

Hat edging

Rnd 1 Using 4mm (USG/6) hook and Peapod and with RS facing, join yarn to brim at beg of rnd, 1ch, work in dc evenly along lower edge, finishing with ss to 1ch to join rnd.

Rnd 2 1ch, 1dc into each st, finishing with ss to 1ch to join rnd.

Fasten off.

gethooked

This is an excellent project to practice double crocheting around an edge (see also page 139). The beauty of crochet is that if you don't like it, you can easily unravel the work and start again.

wool swing jacket

This wool A-line swing coat is ideal for keeping your toddler both warm and looking adorable. It's fastened easily with a snap underneath the chin and finished off with a fun feature button.

Sizes

	1–2 years	2–3 years
Finished chest	24in	28in
	61cm	71cm
Length	13in	14in
	33	35.5cm
Sleeve length	10in	11in
	25.5cm	28cm

Materials

Cornish Organic Wool DK
(230m/251yd per 100g skein)
3[4] x 100g skeins St Breward
(Purple/Heather)
1 large feature button
1 snap fastener
4mm (USG/6) crochet hook

Tension

20 sts x 18 rows over 4in (10cm)
in tweed stitch pattern

Tweed pattern

Foundation row (RS) 1dc into 2nd ch from hook (1ch, miss 1ch, 1dc into next ch) to end.

Row 1 1ch (does not count as st) 1dc into first st, (1dc into each ch sp and 1 ch over each dc) to last st, 1dc into last st.

Rep row 1 for patt.

Swing coat

BACK

Using 4mm (USG/6) hook make 77[89]ch.

Work in tweed stitch patt for 4 rows (including foundation row). 76[88] sts.

Next row (RS) 1ch (does not count as st), dc2tog over 1st 2 sts, patt to last 2 sts, dc2tog over last 2 sts. 74[86] sts Keeping patt correct, dec 1 st at each end of every foll 4th row until 60[71] sts. Work even in patt until back measures 7[7½]in (18[19]cm) ending on a WS row

Shape armholes

Break off yarn. Miss 1st 5 sts, rejoin yarn to next st, patt across to last 5 sts, turn leaving last 5 sts unworked. 50[61] sts. Work even on these sts for a further 6[7½]in (15[19]cm), ending on a WS row.

Shape shoulders

Next Patt 15[18] sts. Fasten off. Miss centre 20[25] sts, rejoin yarn to next st and patt across rem 15[18] sts. Fasten off.

Tweed stitch diagram

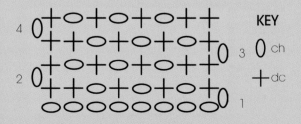

KEY

O ch

+ dc

LEFT FRONT

Using 4mm (USG/6) hook, make 38[44]ch.

Work in tweed stitch patt for 4 rows (including foundation row). 37[43]ch.

Next (RS) 1ch (does not count as st) dc2tog, patt to end, turn. 36[42] sts.

Keeping patt correct, dec 1 st at outer edge of front on every foll 4th row until 30[35] sts.

Work even in Tweed Stitch patt until front measures 7[7½]in (18[19]cm), ending on a WS row.

Shape armhole

Break off yarn, miss 1st 5 sts, rejoin yarn to next st, patt to end 25[30] sts.

Work even in patt on these sts for a further 4in (10cm) ending on a WS row.

Shape neck

Patt to last 6 sts, turn. 19[24] sts.

Dec 1 st on neck edge on every row 4[6] times. 15[18] sts.

Work even in patt until front measures same as back. Fasten off.

RIGHT FRONT

Work as for left front, rev shapings.

SLEEVES (make 2)

Using 4mm (USG/6) hook, make 38[42]ch.

Work in tweed stitch patt for 4 rows (including foundation row). 37[41] sts.

Next (RS) 1ch (does not count as st), 2dc into 1st dc, patt to last st, 2dc into last st. 39[43] sts.

Keeping to patt, cont to inc 1 st at each end of every foll 3rd row until 59[65] sts.

Work even in patt until sleeve measures 10[11]in (25.5[28]cm). Fasten off.

COLLAR (make 2 pieces)

Using 4mm (USG/6) hook, make
40[46]ch.

Work in tweed stitch patt for 2 rows
(including foundation row). 39[45] sts.

Next (RS) 1ch (does not count as st),
2dc into 1st st, patt to last st, 2dc into
last st. 41[47] sts.

Keeping to patt, cont to inc 1 st at
each end of every foll alt row until
50[56] sts. Fasten off.

Sew the 2 collar pieces tog at
one end.

MAKING UP

Darn in loose yarn ends and press
pieces lightly. Join shoulder seams.
Ease collar into place and stitch.
Join sleeves at armhole, then sew
sleeve and side seams.

Front edging

With RS facing, rejoin yarn to left front,
just beneath the collar. Work a row of
double crochet down left front, working
3dc into bottom corner, work across
lower back edge, 3dc into bottom
right corner, work up right front ending
at corner below collar, turn.

Next 1ch, 1dc into each st along
edging, working 3dc into each corner
as before and ending at the top left
front just beneath the collar. Fasten
off and darn in loose yarn ends.
Position the snap fastener centrally
below the collar and sew in place.
Sew button over the fastener.

Cuff edging

With RS facing, rejoin yarn to cuff at
the seam. Work a row of dc around the
cuff, ending with a ss into first dc to join
rnd. Do not turn.

Work a round of crab stitch to finish
(see page 43 for instructions), ending
with a ss to join the rnd.

Fasten off.

gethooked

Instead of a plain double crochet
edging, you could work a row of
picot or crab stitch to add an extra
decorative flourish.

alpaca ribbon shrug

This delicate and pretty little ribbon shrug is ideal as an extra layer for toddler parties. Put it together with your little girl's favourite dress and she's sure to look adorable.

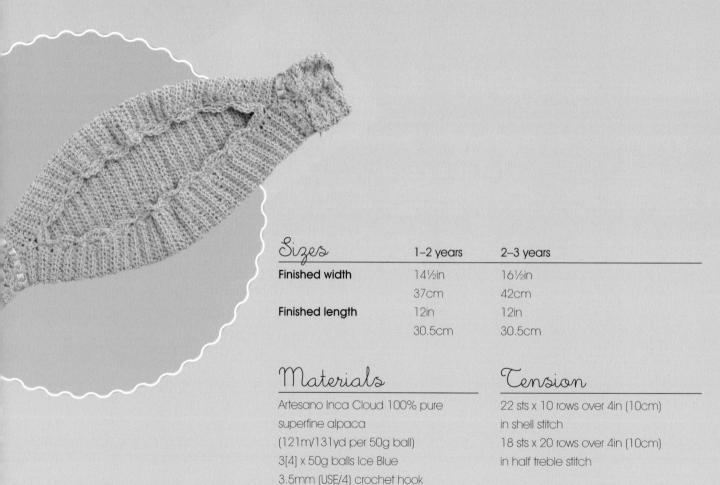

Sizes	1–2 years	2–3 years
Finished width	14½in	16½in
	37cm	42cm
Finished length	12in	12in
	30.5cm	30.5cm

Materials

Artesano Inca Cloud 100% pure
superfine alpaca
(121m/131yd per 50g ball)
3[4] x 50g balls Ice Blue
3.5mm (USE/4) crochet hook
Length of blue ribbon

Tension

22 sts x 10 rows over 4in (10cm)
in shell stitch
18 sts x 20 rows over 4in (10cm)
in half treble stitch

Ribbon shrug

CUFFS (make 2 alike)

Using 3.5mm (USE/4) hook and Ice Blue, make 38(44)ch.

Work shell st as folls:

Foundation row (RS) 1dc into 2nd ch from hook, (miss 2ch, 5tr into next ch, miss 2ch, 1dc into next ch) to end. 37[43] sts.

Row 1 3ch (counts as first tr), 2tr into dc at base of 3ch, (miss 2tr, 1dc into next tr, miss 2tr, 5tr into next dc) to last dc, 3tr into last dc.

Row 2 1ch (does not count as st), 1dc into tr at base of 1ch, (miss 2tr, 5tr into next dc, miss 2tr, 1dc into next tr) to end, working last dc into top of 3ch at beg of prev row.

Rep rows 1–2 once, then rep row 1 once more. Fasten off.

Half treble stitch

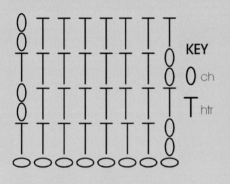

KEY

0 ch

T htr

Shell stitch

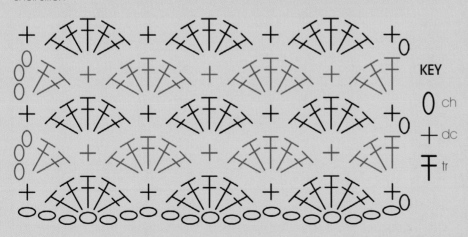

KEY

0 ch

$+$ dc

$\overline{\overline{T}}$ tr

BODY (make 2 alike)

Using 3.5mm (USE/4) hook and Ice Blue, make 32[38]ch.

Row 1 (eyelet row) Miss 2 ch, 1tr into each ch to end. 30[36] sts.

Row 2 2ch, 1htr into each st to end.

Row 3 2ch, 2htr into 1st st, htr across to last st, 2htr into last st. 32[38] sts.

Rep the last 2 rows until there are 54 sts. Work even in htr st until work measures 7¼[8¼]in (18.5[21]cm). Fasten off.

MAKING UP

Darn in loose yarn ends and press pieces lightly. Join the body pieces at centre back (see diagram opposite). Pin cuffs on sleeve ends and sew neatly in place. Sew approx 4in (10cm) of the sleeve seam, working from the cuff towards the centre back. Thread the blue ribbon through the eyelets and tie into a bow.

Edging

Using 3.5mm hook and Ice Blue, join yarn at top edge of shrug at centre back.

Foundation row Work a row of dc evenly around the opening of the shrug, ending with a ss to 1st dc to join rnd.

Row 1 1ch, 1dc into first st, (miss 2 sts, 5tr into next st, miss 2dc, 1dc into next st) to end of rnd, joining with a ss to 1ch to join rnd. Fasten off.

Darn in loose yarn ends.

gethooked

This pattern may not make perfect sense to you until the pieces are complete. Use the assembly diagram to help the making up process and it will fall into place easily.

Shrug assembly diagram

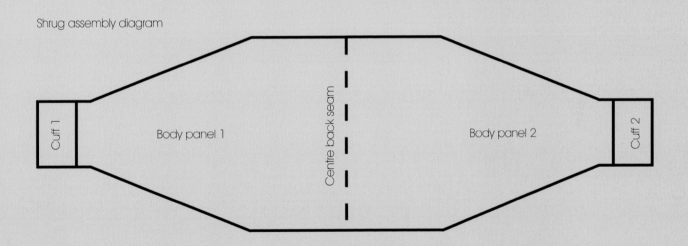

Cuff 1

Body panel 1

Centre back seam

Body panel 2

Cuff 2

wool single-breasted jacket

This classic sports jacket is ideal for casual or occasion wear. It's got proper pockets (essential for storing collections of conkers, stones or string) and smart buttons on the cuffs and front to finish it all off.

Sizes

	1–2 years	2–3 years
Finished chest	28in	30in
	71cm	76cm
Length	14in	15in
	35.5cm	38cm
Sleeve	9in	10in
	23cm	25.5cm

Materials

Sirdar Eco Wool 100% un-dyed virgin wool (100m/109yd per 50g ball)
6[8] x 50g balls in 203 Earth
5 buttons
4mm (USG/6) hook
5 stitch markers

Tension

16 sts x 12 rows over 4in (10cm) in half treble stitch

Buttonholes

Row 1 (WS) 2ch, 1htr into next st, 2ch, miss next 2 sts, 1htr into each st to end.
Row 2 2ch, 1htr into each st (including the 2 ch sts) to end.

Half treble diagram

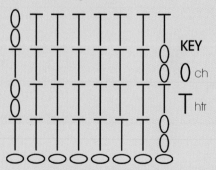

KEY
0 ch
T htr

Jacket

POCKET LININGS (make 2)

Using 4mm (USG/6) hook and Earth, make 14ch.

Foundation row Miss 3ch, 1htr in each ch to end. 12 sts.

Row 1 2ch, 1htr in each st to end. *

Work even (as row 1) until lining measures 3in (8cm).

BACK

Using 4mm (USG/6) hook and Earth, make 58[62]ch.

Foundation row Miss 3ch, 1htr in each ch to end. 56[60] sts.

Row 1 2ch, 1htr in each st to end.

Work even (as row 1) until back measures 8½[9]in (22[23]cm), ending on a RS row. Break off yarn

Shape armholes

(WS) Miss 1st 5 sts, rejoin yarn to next st, 2ch, work 1htr into each of next 46[50] sts, leave last 5 sts unworked. 46[50] sts.

Work even on these sts until armhole measures 5½[6]in (14[15]cm).

Shape neck

Next Work across 14[16] sts, break off yarn, miss centre 18 sts, rejoin yarn to next st, work across rem 14[16] sts. Fasten off.

RIGHT FRONT

Using 4mm (USG/6) hook and Earth, make 34[36]ch.

Foundation row Miss 3ch, 1htr in each ch to end. 32[34] sts.

Row 1 2ch, 1htr in each st to end. Work even (as row 1) until front measures 3in (8cm).

Place pocket

Next row (RS) Work 1st 10[11] sts of right front, 12 sts across top of pocket lining (missing the centre 12 sts of right front), then work rem 10[11] sts of right front. 32[34] sts.

Work even in patt until front measures same as back to armhole, ending on a RS row. Break off yarn.

Shape armhole

(WS) Miss 1st 5 sts, rejoin yarn to next st, 2ch, work 1htr into each of rem 27[29] sts.

Work even on these sts until armhole measures 4[4½]in (10[11.5]cm), ending on a RS row. **

Shape neck

(WS) Patt across 20[22] sts, and turn leaving last 7 sts unworked.

Row 1 2ch, miss 1st htr (to dec), work to end. 19[21] sts.

Row 2 2ch, 1htr in each st to last 2 sts, htr2tog. 18[20] sts.

Rep the last 2 rows until there are 14[16] sts.

Work even until length measures same as back.

Fasten off.

Mark position of 3 buttons (refer to photograph) along edge of right front piece.

LEFT FRONT

Work as for right front to **, but rev all shapings, **and at the same time** make buttonholes to correspond to button markings.

Shape neck

(WS) Ss loosely across 1st 7 sts, 2ch, patt across rem 20[22] sts.

Row 1 2ch, 1htr in each st to last 2 sts, htr2tog. 19[21] sts.

Row 2 2ch, miss 1st htr (to dec), work to end. 18[20] sts.

Rep the last 2 rows until there are 14[16] sts.

Work even until length measures same as back.

Fasten off.

POCKET FLAPS (make 2)

Using 4mm (USG/6) hook and Earth, work as for pocket linings to *, then work even (as row 1) for one more row.

Fasten off.

SLEEVES (make 2)

Using 4mm (USG/6) hook and Earth, make 32[34] ch.

Foundation row Miss 2 ch, 1htr in each ch to end. 30[32] sts.

Rows 1–4 2ch, 1htr in each st to end.

Next (inc row) 2ch, 2htr into first st, 1htr into each st to end, 2htr into last st. 32[34] sts.

Cont in patt, working the inc row on every foll 4th row until there are 44[48] sts.

Then work even until sleeve measures 9[10]in (23[25.5]cm).

Fasten off.

COLLAR

Darn in loose yarn ends and press pieces lightly.

Join shoulder seams.

Place markers at left neck edge inside corner, right neck edge inside corner, and both shoulder seams and centre back. Move markers up as collar progresses.

Row 1 Using 4mm (USG/6) hook and Earth and with RS facing, join yarn at marker at right neck edge inside corner, ch1, work a row of dc evenly around the neck ending at marker at left neck edge inside corner.

Row 2 2ch, 2htr into 1st st, 1htr into each st until 2nd marker (left shoulder), 1tr into marked st, 1htr into each st until 4th marker (right shoulder), 1tr into marked st, 1htr into each st until 5th marker (right neck), 2htr into last st.

Row 3 2ch, 1htr into each st to end.

Row 4 2ch, 2htr into 1st st, 1htr into each st until 2nd marker (left shoulder), 2htr into marked st, 1htr into each st until 3rd marker (centre back), 2htr into marked st, 1htr into each st until 4th marker (right shoulder), 2htr into marked st, 1htr into each st until 5th marker (right neck), 2htr into last st.

Row 5 As row 3.

Row 6 2ch, 1htr into each st until 2nd marker (left shoulder), 2htr into marked st, 1htr into each st until 3rd marker (centre back), 2htr into marked st, 1htr into each st until 4th marker (right shoulder), 2htr into marked st, 1htr into each st until 5th marker (right neck). Fasten off.

MAKING UP

Sew sleeve heads into armholes. Sew sleeve and side seams. Pin pocket linings in place on WS of work and stitch neatly in place. Position pocket flaps and sew in place. Sew one button onto each cuff, and 3 buttons onto jacket front.

gethooked

Make this jacket in organic cotton for a smart, summer version. Sublime Organic DK in Nutmeg would make an ideal substitute.

wool tweed zipped cardigan

This practical cardigan has a zipper up the front for easy fastening. The fronts are worked in simple tweed stitch, but by alternating the three colours; navy, cream and blue, it looks far more complex and your family will think you are a crochet genius.

Sizes

	1–2 years	2–3 years
Finished chest	26in	28in
	66cm	71cm
Length	13in	15in
	33cm	38cm
Sleeve	9in	10in
	23cm	25.5cm

Materials

Cornish Organic Wool DK
(230m/251yd per 100g skein)
2[3] x 100g skeins in St Mawes (Navy)
1 x 100g skein in St Ives (Blue)
1 x 100g skein in Natural
4mm (USG/6) crochet hook
12[14]in (30.5[36]cm) zipper

Tension

16 sts x 8 rows over 4in (10cm)
in treble stitch
20 sts x 18 rows over 4in (10cm)
in multi-coloured tweed stitch

Mock rib pattern

Foundation row (RS) Miss 2 ch (counts as a st), 1htr into each ch to end.

Row 1 2ch (counts as 1st st), miss st at base of 2ch, (1fptr around stem of next st, 1bptr around stem of foll st) to end, with final st around 2ch from prev row. Rep row 1 for patt.

Note the fptr st appears as a bptr st on the reverse and vice versa, in the same way that a purl st in knitting is a knit st on the reverse side.

Mock rib diagram

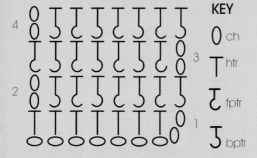

KEY

O ch
T htr
ϡ fptr
ϟ bptr

Treble diagram

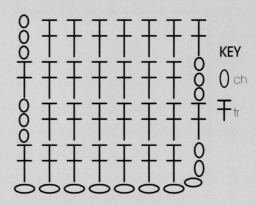

KEY

O ch
T tr

Tweed stitch diagram

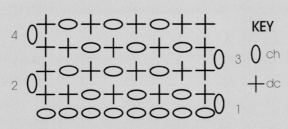

KEY

O ch
+ dc

Jacket

BACK

Using Navy and 4mm (USG/6) hook, make 51[55]ch.

Work foundation row of mock rib. 50[54] sts.

Cont in mock rib until work measures 1½in (4cm).

Next 3ch (counts as st), 1tr into each st to end, turn. 51[55] sts.

Work even in tr st until work measures 7½[9]in (19[23]cm). Break off yarn.

Shape armholes

Miss 1st 4 sts of next row, rejoin yarn to next st, 3ch, tr st across until last 4 sts, turn leaving last 4 sts unworked. 43[47] sts.

Work even on these sts until back measures 13[15]in (33[38]cm).

Shape shoulders

Next 3ch, 1tr into next 13[14] sts. Break off yarn. Miss centre 17[19] sts, rejoin yarn to next st, patt across rem 13[14] sts. Fasten off.

LEFT FRONT

Using Navy and 4mm (USG/6) hook, make 35[37]ch.

Work foundation row of mock rib 34[36] sts.

Work in mock rib until work measures 1½in (4cm).

Body

Begin working multi-coloured tweed stitch as folls:

Row 1 Using Navy, 1ch (does not count as st), 1dc into 1st st, (1ch, miss 1 st, 1dc into foll st) to end, finishing with a dc into t-ch of previous row.

Row 2 Using Cream, 1ch (does not count as st), 1dc into 1st st, (1dc into each ch sp and 1ch over each dc) to last st, 1dc into last st.

Rows 3 and 6 Using Blue, as row 2.

Rows 4 and 7 Using Navy, as row 2.

Row 5 Using Cream, as row 2.

Cont to rep row 2, still alternating Navy, Cream and Blue as set until left front measures 7½[9]in (19[23]cm), ending on a RS row.

Shape armholes

Next patt 30[32] sts, turn.

Work in patt on these sts until armhole measures 4in (10cm).

Shape neck

Next patt 26[28] sts, turn.

Next patt to end, turn.

Next patt 25[27] sts, turn.

Next patt to end, turn.

Rep the last 2 rows, missing the final st at neck edge on every alt row until 21[23] sts rem.

Work even on these st until front measures same as back.

Fasten off.

RIGHT FRONT

Work as for left front, rev all shapings.

SLEEVES

Using 4mm (USG/6) hook and Navy, make 29[33]ch.

Work foundation row of mock rib. 28[32] sts.

Work even in mock rib until cuff measures 1in (2.5cm).

Next 3ch (counts as st), 1tr into each st until end. 29[33] sts.

Rep this row twice more.

Inc row 3ch, 1tr into base of ch,

1tr into each st to last st, 2tr into last st. 31[35] sts.

Work even in tr st, working the inc row on every 4th row until there are 43[47] sts.

Work even on these sts until sleeve measures 9[10]in (23[25.5cm).

MAKING UP

Darn in loose yarn ends and press pieces lightly. Join shoulder seams. Sew sleeve seams, fit to armhole and sew in place. Sew side seams.

Front edging

Using 4mm (USG/6) hook and Navy and with RS facing, rejoin yarn to lower edge of right front and work a row of dc along right front edge, finishing at neck corner, turn.

Next 1ch, 1dc into each st to end. Fasten off.

Rep for left front edge, joining yarn at top neck corner.

Collar

Using 4mm (USG/6) hook and Navy and with RS facing, rejoin yarn to right front neck edge and work a row of dc along right front neck, across back and down left front neck, ending at corner (and ending up with an even number of stitches).

Work in mock rib until collar measures 1.5[2]in (4[5]cm). Fasten off.

Finally, pin zip into place and sew.

gethooked

Always pin and tack your zip in place first so you are sure the teeth won't catch on the wool edging. Then take contrasting sewing thread and back stitch neatly into place.

wool star sweater

This star sweater has become a bit of a classic. Here I have reworked it using crochet. If you struggle with intarsia crochet you could either leave out the star or, still following the chart, try using cross stitch instead.

Sizes

	1–2 years	2–3 years
Finished chest	26in	28in
	66cm	71cm
Length	13in	15in
	33cm	38cm
Sleeve	9in	10in
	23cm	25.5cm

Materials

Cornish Organic Wool DK
(230m/251yd per 100g skein)
2[2] x 100g skeins in St Just (Charcoal)
1[1] x 100g skein in St Eval (Green)
1[1] x 100g skein in Natural
4mm (USG/6) crochet hook

Tension

17 sts x 12 rows over 4in (10cm)
in half treble stitch

Stripe pattern
4 rows Green, 4 rows Natural

Sweater

BACK
Using 4mm (USG/6) hook and Charcoal, make 55[59]ch.

Foundation row (RS) Miss 3ch, 1htr into each ch to end. 53[57] sts.

Row 1 2ch, 1htr into each st to end. * Work even (as row 1) until back measures 7½[9]in (19[23]cm), ending on a WS row. Break off yarn.

Shape armholes
Miss 1st 5 sts, rejoin yarn to next st, 2ch, 1htr into next 43[47] sts, turn leaving last 5 sts unworked. 43[47] sts.
Work even on these sts until back measures 13[15]in (33[38]cm).

Shape shoulders
Next 2ch, 1htr into next 13[14] sts. Break off yarn. Miss centre 17[19] sts, rejoin yarn to next st, 2ch, 1htr into rem 13[14] sts. Fasten off.

FRONT
Work as for back to *, then work even (as row 1) until front measures 4[6]in (10[15]cm).
Beg working from star chart on page 105 as folls:
Next Patt 17[19] sts, work 19 sts of chart, patt 17[19] sts.
Cont as set until front measures 7½[9]in (19[23]cm), ending on WS row. Break off yarn

gethooked
For some different colourways, try using red, white and navy or lilac, pink and cream.

Half treble diagram

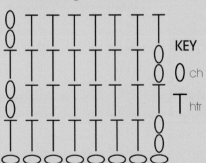

KEY
0 ch
T htr

Shape armholes

Miss 1st 5 sts, rejoin Charcoal to next st, 2ch, 1htr into next 12[14] sts, work 19 sts of chart, 1htr into next 12[14] sts, turn leaving last 5 sts unworked. 43[47] sts.
Cont working even on these sts as set until chart is finished.

Then work even until front measures 10[12]in (25.5[30.5]cm), ending on WS row.

Divide for neck

Row 1 (RS) Patt 20[22] sts, turn.

Row 2 Work even.

Row 3 Patt 11[12] sts, turn.

Cont to work even until length measures same as back. Fasten off.

Second side

With RS facing, miss centre 2 sts, rejoin yarn to next st and patt across rem 20[22] sts, turn.

Cont work to match first side. Fasten off.

SLEEVES (make 2)

Using 4mm (USG/6) hook and Green, make 30[34]ch.

Foundation row Miss 3ch, 1htr into each ch to end. 28[32] sts.

Row 1 2ch, 1htr into each st to end.

Next (inc row) 2ch, 2htr into next st, 1htr into each st until last st, 2htr into last st. 30[34] sts.

Cont to inc on every foll 3rd row until there are 44[48] sts and **at the same time** working in stripe patt.

Then cont to work even in stripe patt until sleeve measures 9[10]in (23[25.5cm). Fasten off.

MAKING UP

Darn in loose yarn ends and press pieces lightly.

Join shoulder seams. Sew sleeve seams, fit to armholes and sew in place. Sew side seams.

Neck edging Using 4mm (USG/6) hook and Charcoal and with RS facing, rejoin yarn to neck edge at shoulder seam. Work a rnd of dc evenly around neck edge, working 3dc into both right and left front corners and working a dc2tog over centre front 2 sts (at the 'V'). Finish with a ss to 1st st to join the rnd.

Cuffs Using 4mm (USG/6) hook and Green and with RS facing, rejoin yarn to sleeve edge at seam. Work a rnd of dc evenly around cuff edge, finishing with a ss to 1st st to join the rnd. Rep for 2nd cuff.

Lower edging Using 4mm (USG/6) hook and Green and with RS facing, rejoin yarn to lower edge at side seam. Work a rnd of dc evenly around whole of lower edge, finishing with a ss to 1st st to join the rnd. Fasten off.

Star chart   19 sts x 16 rows

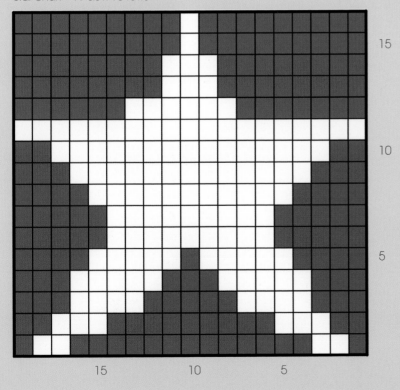

15

10

5

15   10   5

KEY
◼ Charcoal
☐ Natural

Each block = 1 st and 1 row
Read RS rows from R to L and WS rows
from L to R

cotton granny square jacket

In this design I have taken the traditional granny square and used it to edge a contemporary girl's jacket. Worked in the creamy chocolate, strawberry and cream colours of Neapolitan ice cream, this jacket is bound to be a hit.

Sizes

	1–2 years	2–3 years
Finished chest	24½in	28in
	62cm	71cm
Length	13in	14in
	33cm	35.5cm
Sleeve	9in	10in
	23cm	25.5cm

Materials

Sirdar Sublime Organic DK cotton
(110m/120yd per 50g ball)
5[6] x 50g balls in Scumble
1 x 50g ball in Rice Pudding
1 x 50g ball in Nutmeg
4mm (USG/6) crochet hook
Small amount of organic toy stuffing
for buttons
4 pins (to mark button loop placement)

Tension

17 sts x 14 rows over 4in (10cm)
in grit stitch
Each granny square measures 3½in
(9cm) square

Grit stitch pattern

Row 1 Miss 2ch (counts as 1dc), 1tr into next ch, * miss 1ch, work (1dc and 1tr) into next ch, rep from * to last 2ch, miss 1ch, 1dc into last ch.

Row 2 2ch (counts as 1dc), 1tr into first st, * miss 1tr, work (1dc and 1tr) into next dc, rep from * to last 2 sts, miss 1tr, 1dc into top of t-ch.

Rep row 2 for patt.

Jacket

GRANNY SQUARES (make 7[8])

Using 4mm (USG/6) hook and Nutmeg, make 3ch and join with ss to make a ring.

Rnd 1 (RS) 3ch (counts as first tr), 2tr into ring, (2ch, 3tr into ring) 3 times, 2ch, 1ss into top of 3ch at beg of rnd.
Change to Scumble and join yarn to a 2ch corner sp.

Rnd 2 3ch (counts as first tr), (2tr, 2ch, 3tr) into 2ch corner sp, * 2ch, miss 3tr, (3tr, 2ch and 3tr) into 2ch corner sp, rep from * twice more, 2ch, miss 3tr, 1ss into top of 3ch at beg of rnd.
Change to Rice Pudding and join yarn to a 2ch corner sp.

Rnd 3 3ch (counts as first tr), (2tr, 2ch, 3tr) into 2ch corner sp, ** 2ch, miss 3tr, 3tr in 2ch sp, 2ch, miss 3tr, (3tr, 2ch, 3tr) into 2ch corner sp, rep from ** twice more, 2 ch, miss 3tr, 3tr in 2ch sp, 2ch,

Grit stitch diagram

KEY

O ch

+ dc

T tr

1ss into top of 3ch at beg of rnd. Change to Scumble and join yarn to a 2ch corner sp.

Rnd 4 (2dc into each 2ch sp, 1dc in each tr) to end of rnd. Break off yarn. Fasten off. Darn in loose yarn ends.

JACKET BODY (worked in one piece)

Using 4mm (USG/6) hook and Scumble, make 107[123]ch.

Work row 1 of grit stitch pattern. 105[121] sts.

Work row 2 and cont to work even in grit stitch until body measures 4½[5]in (11.5[13]cm), ending with RS facing for next row.

Shape right front

Next Patt 24[28], turn.

Work even on these 24[28] sts until left front measures 3in (8cm), ending on a WS row.

Next Patt 18[22] sts, turn.

Next Patt to end.

Next Patt 17[21] sts.

Next Patt to end.

Next Patt 16[20] sts.

Next Patt to end.

2nd size only:

Next Patt 19 sts, turn.

Next Patt to end.

Next Patt 18 sts, turn.

Next Patt to end.

Both sizes

Work even in patt until armhole measures 5[5½]in (13[14]cm).

Fasten off.

Back

With RS facing, miss next 4 sts, rejoin yarn to next st, patt 49[57] sts.

Work even on these sts until back measures 1 row less than left front.

Shape neck

Next Patt 16[18] sts, break off yarn. Miss centre 17[21] sts, rejoin yarn to next st, patt to end.

Fasten off.

Left front

With RS facing, miss next 4 sts, rejoin yarn to next st and patt across rem 24[28] sts.

Work as for right front, rev all shapings.

SLEEVES (make 2 alike)

Using 4mm (USG/6) hook and Scumble, make 33[37]ch.

Work foundation row of grit stitch. 31[35] sts.

Rows 1–4 Work as row 2 (patt row) of grit stitch.

Next (inc row) 2ch (counts as 1dc), 1dc and 1tr into first st (1 st increased), miss 1tr, work (1dc and 1tr) into next dc, rep from * to last 2 sts, miss 1tr, 1dc and 1tr into top of tch (2nd st increased). 33[37] sts.

Keeping to patt, cont to work the inc row on every foll 4th row until 43[47] sts.

Work even until sleeve measures 9[10] in (23[25.5]cm).

Fasten off.

MAKING UP

Sew sleeve seams. Fit to armholes on body and sew in place.

Take the granny squares and using your 4mm (USG/6) hook and Scumble, join them along each side edge with a row of dc. You will have one long strip of squares. Line these up at the bottom edge of the jacket and either sew neatly in place or use a row of dc to attach as before.

Cuff edging

Using 4mm (USG/6) hook and Scumble and with RS facing, join yarn at seam, 1ch, work a row of dc evenly around cuff edging, finishing with a ss to 1ch to join the rnd.

Next (Picot edging) (3ch, 1dc into base of ch, 1dc into next 2dc,) rep to end of rnd, finishing with a ss to join the rnd.

Fasten off.

Jacket edging

Using 4mm (USG/6) hook and Scumble and with RS facing, join yarn at neck at right shoulder, 1ch, work round of dc evenly around whole of jacket edge, working 3dc at both front collar edges and also at lower front corners, finishing with a ss to 1ch to join the rnd.

Fasten off.

Buttons (make 2)

Using 4mm (USG/6) hook and Nutmeg make 2ch.

Row 1 (RS) 5dc into 2nd ch from hook. Close this and every foll rnd with a ss into 1st ch to join the rnd.

Row 2 1ch, 2dc into each st. 10 sts.

Row 3 1ch, 1dc into each st.

Row 4 1ch, (1dc, miss 1dc) 5 times. 5 sts.

Fasten off.

Pack the centre of the button with a little toy stuffing. Cut yarn leaving a long tail to gather up the 5 sts and close opening.

Sew both buttons in position.

Button loops

Mark position of button loops on right front edge with 4 pins (2 pins per button – one each to mark either end of button loop).

Using 4mm (USG/6) hook and Scumble, join yarn to 1st marker. Make 4ch, join ch to edge of jacket at 2nd marker with a ss, turn.

Next Work 8 dc across button loop chain, finishing back at 1st marker with a ss to jacket edge.

Fasten off.

Rep for 2nd button loop.

gethooked

If you are struggling with crochet buttons, try a conventional button instead. A small pearl-style button would look just as good.

PART THREE

Accessories

soya & cotton nappy pants

Known as soakers in the US, these practical adjustable nappy covers are adorable. I've worked on the premise that baby may be crawling, so all the detail is on the bottom!

Sizes

	small	medium	large
To fit hips up to	18in	22in	24in
	46cm	56cm	61cm
Rise from bottom of gusset	7½in	9in	10in
	19cm	23cm	25.5cm

Materials

FRILLY PANTS
Sirdar F088 Just Soya 100% natural soya (105m/115yd per 50g ball)
3 x 50g balls in Raspberry Tea
2 buttons

SPOTTY PANTS
Sirdar Sublime Organic DK cotton (approx 110m/120yd per 50g ball)
2 x 50g balls in Rice Pudding
1 x 50g ball in Clay
1 x 50g ball in Nutmeg
1 x 50g ball in Peapod

FOR BOTH STYLES
4mm (USG/6) crochet hook
4 snap fasteners
10in (25cm) elastic
Sewing thread and needle

Tension

18 sts x 22 rows over 4in (10cm) in double crochet

Double crochet

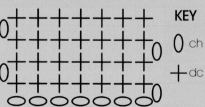

KEY

O ch

+ dc

Nappy pants

Work this pattern for both designs, using either Raspberry Tea for frilly pants or Rice Pudding for spotty pants.

BODY

Using 4mm (USG/6) hook, make 43[53:57]ch.

Foundation row 1dc into 2nd ch from hook, 1dc into each ch to end. 42[52:56] sts.

Row 1 1ch, 1dc into each st to end. Work even (as row 1) until work measures 4[5:6]in (10[13:15]cm).

Shape legs and gusset

Next (dec row) 1ch, miss 1st dc, 1dc into each st to last 2 sts, dc2tog. 40[50:54]dc.

Cont working in dc, but dec as set on every foll alt row until 32[42:46] sts. Then work even in dc until work measures 7½[9:10]in (19[23:25.5]cm).

Next (inc row) 1ch, 2dc into 1st st, 1dc into each st until last st, 2dc into last st. 34[44:48] sts.

Cont working in dc, but inc as set on every foll alt row until 42[52:56] sts. Work even until work measures 15[18:20]in (38[46:51]cm).

Fasten off. Darn in loose yarn ends. Fold pants in half, matching each waistband. Pin and sew side seams working from waist top down to the top of the leg openings.

DECORATION

Frilly pants

Make 5 frilly ruffles along the back of pants as folls:

Foundation row Using 4mm (USG/6) hook and Raspberry Tea, work a row of dc evenly across the surface of the pants from one side of the leg opening to the other, turn.

Row 1 1ch, 2dc into each st to end.

Row 2 1ch, 1dc into each st to end. Fasten off.

Space the rem 4 frills equally along the back.

Spotty pants

Small spots (make 4 in Nutmeg, 2 in Clay, 1 in Peapod)

Using 4mm (USG/6) hook, make 2ch.

Foundation rnd Work 5dc into 2nd ch from hook, ss to 1st dc to join rnd.

Rnd 1 1ch, 2dc into each dc to end, ss to 1st ch to join rnd *.

Fasten off, leaving a long tail.

Large spots (make 2 in Peapod, 1 in Nutmeg, 1 in Clay)

Work as for small spots to *.

Rnd 2 1ch, (1dc into next st, 2dc into foll st) 5 times. 15 sts. Fasten off, leaving a long tail.

Reserve 2 small nutmeg spots for front flaps. Position the remaining spots over the back of the pants and sew in with the long tail and a tapestry needle.

LEG OPENINGS

Frilly pants

Foundation rnd Using 4mm (USG/6) hook and Raspberry Tea, work a rnd of dc evenly around first leg opening, ss to 1st dc to join rnd.

Rnd 1 1ch, 2dc into each st to end, ss to 1st ch to join rnd.

Rnd 2 1ch, 1dc into each st to end, ss to 1st ch to join rnd.

Rnd 3 2ch, 2htr into each st to end, ss to top of t-ch to join rnd.
Fasten off.
Rep for second leg.

Spotty pants

Foundation rnd Using 4mm (USG/6) hook and Nutmeg, work a rnd of dc evenly around first leg opening, ss to 1st dc to join rnd.

Rnd 1 2ch, 1htr into each st to end, ss to top of t-ch to join rnd.
Rep row 1 once. Fasten off.
Fold leg edging in half and slip stitch in place to inside edge of leg opening.
Rep for second leg.

WAISTBAND (both styles)

Using 4mm (USG/6) hook and either Raspberry Tea for frilly pants or Rice Pudding for spotty pants, make 44ch.

Foundation row 1htr into 3rd ch from hook, 1htr into each ch to end. 42 sts.

Row 1 2ch, 1htr into each st to end.
Fasten off.

Take your elastic and attach in place to back of pants as folls:

Using sewing thread, sew one end firmly to first side edge, then cover the elastic with a row of herringbone stitches. Leave the other end unstitched for the moment and do not draw up elastic.

Place the waistband casing over the top of the elastic. Slip stitch in place along top and bottom.

Now draw up your elastic until pants are the right size. Sew the other end of the elastic firmly in place and snip off excess. Slip stitch both ends of waistband casing in place.

FRONT FLAPS (both styles)

Using 4mm (USG/6) hook and either Raspberry Tea for frilly pants or Rice Pudding for spotty pants, make 5ch.

Foundation row 1dc into 2nd ch from hook, 1dc into each ch to end. 4 sts.

Row 1 1ch, 2dc into 1st st, 1dc into each st to end. 5 sts.

Row 2 1ch, 1dc into each st to end.

Rep rows 1–2 until there are 8 sts.
Work row 2 once more. Fasten off.
Rep for 2nd flap.
Work a row of dc evenly around the
edge of each flap, working 3dc into
each corner. Fasten off.
Position both flaps at opposite front
side edges. Sew in place with
narrowest tips facing towards the
middle point of pants.
Sew a snap onto the underside of
each flap at the narrowest point.
Sew a button on the upper edge for
frilly pants and a Nutmeg spot for the
spotty pants.
Take 4 opposite popper fastenings
(2 for each flap). Position the first 2
so that the pants are at their widest
fitting when the flaps are in place.
Sew firmly to front waist.
Now take the other 2 poppers and
position them to the centre of the front
waist so the pants are drawn up when
the flaps are in place. Sew them firmly
in place.

gethooked

Seriously, the bottom is where
it's at with these pants! Use
embroidery, intarsia, stripes and
sequins to personalize your little
cherub's derrière!

soya nursing cushion cover

A V-shaped cushion is an essential item for any nursing mother. I've designed this cover using the softest soya yarn in calm, harmonious colours. Its button fastening makes it easy to remove and wash so feeding times can be shared in total comfort.

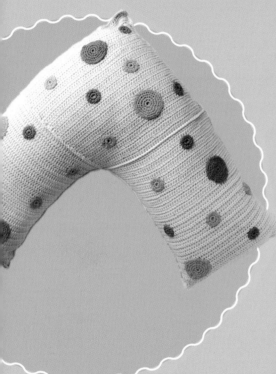

Materials

Sirdar F088 Just Soya 100% natural soya (105m/115yd per 50g)
9 x 50g balls in Vanilla Pod
1 x 50g ball in Raspberry Tea
1 x 50g ball in Soya Blue
5 buttons (by Stockwell Pottery, see *Suppliers* page 142)
4mm (USG/6) crochet hook

Size

To fit a standard size nursing cushion
Square 13in (33cm) square
Rectangle 13in x 15in (33cm x 38cm)

Half treble

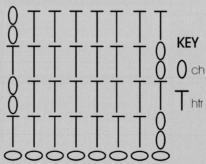

KEY
O ch
T htr

Tension

17 sts x 20 rows over 4in (10cm) in half treble stitch

Cushion cover

SQUARES (make 2)

Using 4mm (USG/6) hook and Vanilla Pod, make 57ch.
Foundation row Miss 3 ch, 1htr into each ch to end. 55 sts.
Row 1 2ch, 1htr into each st to end *. Rep row 1 until square measures 13in (33cm).
Fasten off.

RECTANGLES (make 4)

Work as for square to *.
Rep row 1 until square measures 15in (38cm).
Fasten off.

LARGE SPOTS (make 3 in Soya Blue and 3 in Raspberry Tea)

Using 4mm (USG/6) hook make 4ch.

Ss to 1st ch to join the rnd.

Rnd 1 1ch, work 10 dc into circle.

Rnd 2 (2dc into each st) to end. 20 sts. *

Rnd 3 (1dc into next st, 2dc into foll st) to end. 30 sts.

Rnd 4 (1dc into each of next 2 sts, 2dc into foll st) to end. 40 sts.

Rnd 5 (1dc into each of next 3 sts, 2dc into foll st) to end. 50 sts.

Rnd 6 (1dc into each of next 4 sts, 2dc into foll st) to end. 60 sts.
Fasten off.

SMALL SPOTS (make 9 in Soya Blue and 9 in Raspberry Tea)
Work as for large spot to *.
Fasten off.

MAKING UP
Darn in loose yarn ends.
Following the diagram, join all the squares using double crochet with 4mm (USG/6) hook and Vanilla Pod. Arrange the spots randomly across the front of the cushion and slip stitch neatly in place.

Buttonband
Using 4mm (USG/6) hook and Vanilla Pod, make 56ch.

Foundation row 1dc into 2nd ch from hook, 1dc into each ch to end. 55 sts.

Rows 1–2 1ch, 1dc into each st to end.

Buttonhole row (RS) 1ch, 1dc into

each of next 5 sts, (make 2 ch and miss 2 sts, 1dc in each of next 9 sts) 4 times, make 2 ch and miss 2 sts, 1dc in each of next 4 sts.

Row 5 1ch, 1dc into each st and ch to end. Fasten off.

Darn in loose yarn ends and sew button band in place on lower edge.

Buttons
Sew the 5 buttons along the lower edge, to corresp with buttonholes (see diagram below).

Square	Rectangle
Rectangle Leave this lower edge open when joining pieces with double crochet Buttons positioned on upper side. o o o o o	Cushion cover assembly diagram (back and front alike)

cotton cot mobile

This cute cot mobile is deceptively simple to make. Just attach to a hook above your baby's head and watch their eyes follow the spinning frog as he chases after the bug on the flowers.

Materials

Sublime Organic DK cotton
(approx 110m/120yd per 50g ball)
1 x 50g ball in Peapod
1 x 50g ball in Clay
1 x 50g ball in Rice Pudding
1 x 50g ball in Nutmeg
1 x 50g ball in Scumble
Scraps of black yarn for embroidery
4mm (USG/6) crochet hook
The inner ring from an 8in (20.5cm)
embroidery hoop
Pack of bugs and blossom buttons
Cornish organic toy stuffing
Length of lime green ribbon

Tension

Not critical

Hoop cover

Using 4mm (USG/6) hook and Nutmeg,
make 6ch.
Foundation row Miss 1ch, 1dc into
each ch to end. 5 sts.
Row 1 1ch, 1dc into each st to end.
Rep row 1 until work is long enough
to cover the circumference of the
embroidery hoop with a slight stretch.
Fasten off.
Fold in half lengthwise and pin in place
around the hoop. Sew the seam with
a firm slip stitch.

Flowers

(make 2 – one with Clay petals and
Scumble centre, and the other with
Scumble petals and Clay centre)

PETALS (5 per flower)
Using 4mm (USG/6) hook, make 2ch.
Work 5dc into 2nd ch from hook, ss to
1st dc to join rnd. 5 sts.

Row 1 1ch, 2dc into each st, ss to 1ch to join rnd. 10 sts. *

Row 2 1ch, 1dc into each of next 3 sts, 2htr in next st, 3tr in each of next 2 sts, 3dtr in next st, 3tr in each of next 2 sts, 2htr in foll st, ss to 1ch to join rnd. Fasten off.

FLOWER CENTRE

(make 2 for each flower)
Using 4mm (USG/6) hook, work as for petals to *.

Row 2 1ch, (1dc into next st, 2dc in foll st) 5 times, ss to 1ch to join rnd. 15 sts.

Row 3 1ch (1dc into each of next 2 sts, 2dc in foll st) 5 times, ss to 1ch to join rnd. 20 sts. **
Fasten off.

MAKING UP

Lay the first flower centre on a flat surface. Position the petals around the edge, overlapping the petal edges with the centre slightly. Place a layer of stuffing in the centre of the flower and lay the second flower centre over the top to make a sandwich of petals and stuffing. Pin in place and sew around the edge of the flower centre, making sure to catch each layer firmly. Take a bug button and sew in place to one of the petals.

Frogs (make 2)

BODY

Using 4mm (USG/6) hook and Peapod, make 2ch.
Work as for flower centre to **

Row 4 1ch, (1dc into each of next 3 sts, 2dc in foll st) 5 times, ss to join rnd. 25 sts.

Row 5 1ch, (1dc in each of next 4 sts, 2dc in foll st) 5 times, ss to join rnd. 30 sts. ***
Mark position of next st with some contrast yarn so you know where the beg of each rnd is.

Row 6 1ch, 1dc into each st, ss to join rnd.

Rows 7–10 As row 6.

Row 11 1ch, (1dc into each of next 4 sts, dc2tog) 5 times, ss to join rnd. 25 sts.

Row 12 1ch, (1dc into each of next 3 sts, dc2tog) 5 times, ss to join rnd. 20 sts.

Row 13 1ch, (1dc into each of next 2 sts, dc2tog) 5 times, ss to join rnd. 15 sts.

Row 14 1ch, (1dc into next st, dc2tog) 5 times, ss to join rnd. 10 sts.
At this point, stuff your frog firmly with toy stuffing as the hole may become too small later.

Row 15 1ch, (dc2tog) 5 times, finish with a ss to join rnd. 5 sts.

Fasten off, leaving a long tail.
Thread the tail onto a tapestry needle
and run a row of gathering stitches
around the opening and pull tight.
Secure with a few stitches and snip
the yarn.

EYES (make 2 for each frog)

Using 4mm (USG/6) hook and Rice
Pudding, make 2ch.
Work 5dc into 2nd ch from hook,
ss to 1st dc to join rnd.
Row 1 1ch, (2dc into each st) to end,
ss to 1ch to join rnd. 10 sts *.
Row 2 1ch, (1dc into next st, 2dc in foll
st) 5 times, ss to join rnd. 15 sts.
Fasten off.
Round the eye shape (like a contact
lens) and stuff inner with a small piece
of stuffing.
Place on top of the frog's head (see
photo) and sew in place. Use a small
amount of black yarn to embroider the
eye with satin stitches.
Rep for the other eye.
Take the black yarn and embroider
the mouth using back stitch. Sew a
bug button in place at one corner
of the mouth.

LEGS (make 2 for each frog)

Using 4mm (USG/6) hook and Peapod,
work as for frog eyes to *.
Now work 12ch, turn.
Work 1dc into 2nd ch from hook and
then another dc into the foll ch.
Fasten off.
Sew each leg in place to the lower
part of frog body (see photo).

Lily pad

Using 4mm (USG/6) hook and Peapod,
work as for frog's body to ***.
Next 2ch, 2htr into each of next 6 sts,
1dc in each of next 18 sts, 2htr in each
of foll 6 sts, turn. 42 sts.
Next 3ch, 1tr into each of next 6 sts,
1htr in each of next 5 sts, 1dc in each
of next 20 sts, 1htr in each of next 5 sts,
1tr in each of foll 6 sts. Fasten off.
Sew 3 flower buttons to the lily pad.

Making up

You need to make four chains to hang your frogs and flowers. Use a 4mm (USG/6) hook and Rice Pudding. However, I would say, this is not an exact science and the finished mobile has to end up weighted evenly so it hangs straight from the hook. My finished chains were around about 17in (43cm) in length but I played around a bit because I wanted each flower and frog to differ slightly in the heights at which they hung.

Attach the yarn to the top of your frog's head or flower petal and secure with a slip stitch. Now work the chain to about 17in (43cm). Do this for all the flowers and frogs. Now play about with their position on the hoop. You need to wind the chains around the hoop, leaving enough length at the top for each strand to meet in the middle. Everything should hang evenly and not pull the hoop over to one side. If this happens, slide the frog or flower a little around the hoop until you get it just right.

Now secure your chains to the hoop with a knot. Take the upper strands and pull them together at the top of the hoop. Tie them in a knot. Your mobile should now hang perfectly when you hold it up from this knot.

Using a 4mm (USG/6) hook and Rice Pudding, make a ch 5in (13cm) in length. Fasten off. Fold this in half to make a hanging hook and sew in place to the top knot. Take your green ribbon and make a floppy bow. Use the ribbon and the lily pad to disguise these knots. Place them over the top and sew neatly in place with a few stitches.

gethooked

You could make a version of this mobile in black, white and red. Young babies' eyes can focus easily on these colours.

wool soother holders

These soother holders clip onto baby's jacket or pram with a safety pin and fasten securely to the dummy with a button. Ideal for using up leftover scraps of DK yarn, they are a fun way of keeping those beloved soothers from ending up on the floor.

Materials

Cornish Organic Wool DK
(230m/251yd per 100g skein)
1 x 100g skein St Just (Charcoal)
1 x 100g skein St Hilary (Amber)
1 x 100g skein St Breward (Purple)
1 x 100g skein St Blazey (Pink)
1 x 100g skein St Eval (Green)
1 x 100g skein Natural
Cornish organic toy stuffing
4mm (USG/6) crochet hook
Fabric glue
Small scraps of white, blue and
purple felt
2 small buttons
2 nappy pins with the locking head
(for safety when attaching to little ones)
2 dummies with a ring attachment

Tension

Not critical

Bumble bee

BODY

Using 4mm (USG/6) hook and Charcoal, make 2ch.
Work 5dc into 2nd ch from hook, ss to 1st dc to join rnd.

Rnd 1 Mark 1st st with coloured thread so you know where each rnd starts and ends, 1ch, 2dc into each of next 5dc. 10 sts.

Rnds 2–4 1dc into each st.

Rnd 5 Change to Amber, (1dc in next st, 2dc into foll st) 5 times. 15 sts.

Rnd 6 Change to Charcoal, (1dc in each of next 2 sts, 2dc into foll st) 5 times. 20 sts.

Rnd 7 Change to Amber, 1dc into each st.

Rnd 8 Change to Charcoal, (1dc in next 2 sts, dc2tog) 5 times. 15 sts.

Rnd 9 Change to Amber, (1dc, dc2tog) 5 times. 10 sts.

Rnds 10–11 Using Charcoal, 1dc into each st.

At this point, stuff your bee with organic

stuffing firmly as the next row will close the opening so you might not be able to fill your toy adequately.

Rnd 12 (Dc2tog) 5 times. 5 sts.

Fasten off leaving a long tail.

Now, push a little more stuffing through the small hole if necessary. Then thread the long tail onto a tapestry needle and run a row of gathering stitches around the opening and pull tight. Fasten off and darn in loose ends.

WINGS (make 2)

Using 4mm (USG/6) hook and Natural, make 2ch.

Work 5dc into 2nd ch from hook, ss to 1st dc to join rnd.

Rnd 1 1ch, 2dc into each of next 5 sts, ss to 1ch to join rnd. 10 sts.

Rnd 2 1ch, 1dc into each of next 3 sts, 2htr into each of next 2 sts, 2tr into each of next 3 sts, 2htr into each of next 2 sts, ss to 1ch to join rnd.

Fasten off.

Darn in loose yarn ends.

Position wings at back of bee's body and stitch neatly in place.

ANTENNAE (make 2)

Thread a length of Charcoal yarn onto a tapestry needle.

Fasten to top of bee's head above one eye, thread through and leaving a long tail, snip the thread. Tie a knot in the top of the thread.

EYES

Using a scrap of white and blue felt and using the photo for reference, snip 2 white eyes and 2 blue irises. Secure to bee's face with dabs of fabric glue.

PIN FASTENING

Secure your nappy pin to the back of your bee with some firm stitches. Take a piece of white felt, cut out a circle big enough to cover the sewn part of the pin. Lay it in place and slip stitch around the edge to secure.

Soother holder

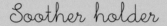

Using 4mm (USG/6) needle and Charcoal, make 32ch.

Next 1htr into 3rd ch from hook, 1htr into each ch to end. Fasten off.

Darn in loose yarn ends.

Sew one end to the base of your bumble bee.

Fold up the bottom of the soother holder and position the button.

Sew button firmly in place. Use one of the half trebles as a buttonhole.

Attach your dummy and secure with the button.

Butterfly

UPPER WINGS (make 2)

Using 4mm (USG/6) hook and Pink, make 2ch.

Work 5dc into 2nd ch from hook, ss to 1st dc to join rnd. 5 sts.

Rnd 1 Change to Green, 1ch, 2dc into each of next 5 sts, ss to 1ch to join the rnd. 10 sts.

Rnd 2 Change to Purple *, 1ch, 1dc into each of next 3 sts, 2htr into next st, 3tr into each of next 2 sts, 3dtr into next st, 3tr into next 2 sts, 2htr into next st, ss to 1ch to join the rnd. Fasten off.

LOWER WINGS (make 2)

Work as for upper wings to *.

Next 1ch, (1dc in next st, 2dc into foll st) 5 times. 15 sts.

Fasten off.

BODY

Using 4mm (USG/6) hook and Green, make 3ch.

Row 1 1dc into 2nd ch from hook, 1dc, turn. 2 sts.

Row 2 1ch, 2dc into each st. 4 sts.

Row 3 As row 2. 8 sts.

Rows 4–8 1ch, 1dc into each st.

Row 9 (Dc2tog) 4 times. 4 sts.

Row 10 (Dc2tog) twice. 2 sts.

Next Dc2tog.

Fasten off, leaving a long tail.

Using a tapestry needle, thread the long tail end and sew up rear seam of body. Sew body with organic stuffing as you go until he is cocoon-shaped. Fasten off.

MAKING UP

Position upper wings at upper rear of butterfly body. Sew in place. Now, position lower wings and sew these in place. Work antennae as for bee using Green yarn. Add eyes as for bumble bee. Fix the pin as for bumble bee using a circle of purple felt. Finally, work the holder as for bumble bee using Green yarn.

gethooked

My daughter loves her dummy so
much that I have made her several
versions of this soother holder.
Try using the flower from the cot
mobile on page 122 in place of
the bee or butterfly.

PART FOUR

Crochet basics

getting started

Buying yarn

It is a good idea to buy the actual yarns specified in my patterns. In this way you will be sure the finished garment will look every bit as good as the picture. Details of suppliers are included at the back of the book. Do try contacting them online if you are not sure where to purchase a specific yarn type. Their sales department will be able to put you in contact with your local stockist or online supplier so you should find it a relatively straightforward process to match everything up.

DYE LOTS

Remember, yarn is always dyed in batches or lots so when purchasing, always check the dye lot on the ball band carefully. Make sure all the numbers match, otherwise your finished garment might turn out to be a disappointment if there is colour variation when you change balls. This is even more important when selecting yarn dyed using organic colours where the finished product can vary quite significantly from batch to batch. Make sure you order plenty of the same dye lot and ask for a 'lay-by' service if you're not sure of your amounts.

SUBSTITUTION

If you choose to substitute the yarns recommended on the pattern there are several pointers to bear in mind. Firstly, always choose the same weight yarn to substitute with i.e. double knit, chunky, Aran etc.

Secondly, check the yardage on your preferred yarn. It will be written on the ball band. There may be less or more per ball than on the recommended type. In this case, you will need to allow for extra or fewer balls, so take time to work it out carefully.

Finally, always crochet a tension swatch in your substitute yarn before beginning the project. You need to do this to check the stitch sizes match and the finished garment will come out the correct size. Also, it will give you a better idea of how the whole thing is going to look.

Sizing

The sizes for each garment are given at the beginning of every pattern. I have tried to include a wide range of sizes appropriate to each project. However, all babies vary in size so don't be afraid to alter sleeve and sweater lengths if necessary.

Tension swatches

In order to ensure success when crocheting, you must obtain the correct gauge or tension. The quick way to check your tension is the same as stated in the pattern is to crochet a tension square about 6in (15cm) wide in the same pattern stitch and with the correct yarn and hook size. When you have completed it, lay the square down flat and measure it, vertically and horizontally. If your square has too few stitches or rows then your tension is too loose and you should try again with a smaller hook size. If it has too many stitches, try a larger hook.

Following patterns

Before you begin crocheting, always read the pattern through from beginning to end. It's a good idea to underline the size you are crocheting throughout the pattern. That way, you know exactly where you are at a glance. Figures for larger sizes are given in square brackets and where only one figure appears, this applies to all sizes. Next, check any abbreviations you are not sure of against the list on page 141 and, just like following a recipe, gather all your yarn, tools and notions together before you start.

Stitch diagrams

Stitch diagrams are detailed maps of the actual crochet stitches. They let you see exactly where you are and what you are going to do on each row. You will need to know which symbol represents which stitch and therefore you should familiarize yourself with the key before starting. Once you are familiar with them (they are a universal language) then you will quickly get used to these diagrams and may prefer using them to written instructions.

Reading charts

Some of my patterns use intarsia charts. As in all knitting and crochet charts, one square represents one stitch and one line of squares is equal to one row.

On right side rows, read the chart from right to left and on wrong side rows, do the opposite i.e. read from left to right. Begin crocheting from the bottom right side corner of the chart at Row 1. Carry on to Row 2 and 3 and so on until the chart is complete.

You will see that every square has either a symbol or colour marked on it. Read the accompanying key to understand which colour or stitch you need to use to complete the row.

A chart ruler (available from most good haberdashers or yarn stores) is an excellent investment. You can clip it onto the chart and move it up or down the rows once you've completed it. That way you won't get muddled or lost in the middle.

basic techniques

HOLDING THE HOOK

There are several ways to hold your crochet hook comfortably. Personally, I hold my hook in the right hand and wield it a little like a knitting needle, feeding the yarn from my right hand just like I do when I am knitting. However, I am self-taught and this is not the traditional way to use your hook and I am sure it is far clumsier than the 'proper' method which I shall outline below. But at the end of the day, whatever works for you is all that is important. As long as you are making stitches, that's the main thing!

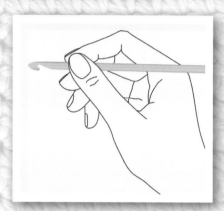

1 Hold the hook in your right hand as if it were a pencil.

2 With your left hand facing you with fingers spread out slightly, hook the yarn over the back of your little finger, under your palm and then back over the top of your index finger. Your left hand is now holding the yarn and is also free to hold the piece of fabric as it is being worked. Hold your crochet hook in your right hand and begin work.

MAKING A CHAIN

Most crochet you do will start with a chain. Make sure you always make the correct number of chains stated and ensure they are not too tight. This will make the first row much easier to complete successfully. So, you are holding your yarn in your left hand and hook with slip knot on it in your right:

1 Hold the tail of the slip knot firmly with your left hand and catch the yarn with your hook and draw it back through the loop of your slip knot. This completes your first chain.

2 Repeat this action, drawing your yarn back through the loop of the previous chain to complete the number of chains stated on your pattern.

3 A basic chain shown from the front.

4 A basic chain shown from the back.

SLIP STITCH

This stitch is used to join a round or to move across rows without making tall stitches.

1 Slip your crochet hook under the top two strands of the 'V' of the first stitch of the row.

2 Catch your yarn with your hook and draw it back through both 'V' and the loop on the hook.

DOUBLE CROCHET

This is one of the most common crochet stitches and forms a thick, tight fabric. You will need to make a turning chain of one stitch at the beginning of every row.

1 Insert the hook under both strands of the 'V' in the second stitch from the hook. Catch the yarn with your hook and draw it back through the 'V'.

2 You should now have two loops on your hook. Now catch the yarn again with your hook and draw it back through both loops on the hook.

HALF TREBLE CROCHET

This is a slightly taller stitch than the double crochet. You will need to make a turning chain of two stitches at the beginning of every row.

1 Make your turning chain. Wind your yarn around the nose of your hook once before inserting it under both 'V' strands of the first stitch of the row.

2 Now wind your yarn around the nose of your hook once again and draw the hook back through the 'V'. You should now have three loops on your hook. Wind your yarn around the nose of your hook again and draw the hook back through all of the three loops.

TREBLE CROCHET

This is an even taller stitch than the half treble stitch. You will need to make a turning chain of three stitches at the beginning of every row.

1 Make your turning chain. Wind your yarn around the nose of your hook once before inserting it under both 'V' strands of the first stitch of the row.

2 Now wind your yarn around the nose of your hook once again and draw the hook back through the 'V'. You should now have three loops on your hook.

3 Wind your yarn around the nose of your hook and draw it back through only two of those loops. Now you have only two loops on your hook.

4 Wind your yarn around the nose of your hook for a final time and draw it back through both loops. You have one loop left on your hook.

INCREASING

Increasing stitches within your piece of crochet is incredibly easy. You can add stitches anywhere across your row, although it is probably more common to find increases at the beginning and ends of rows.

All you have to do is to make two stitches into the same stitch. It's as simple as that. The pattern will tell you which stitch to use and where to make the increase.

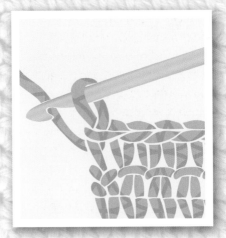

DECREASING

To decrease in crochet you can either miss out a stitch altogether i.e. skip it; in which case the pattern will tell you exactly which stitches to skip and when. Or you can work two stitches together so they become one.

This is quite straightforward to do and these decreases are described as follows:

DC2 TOG or double crochet decrease

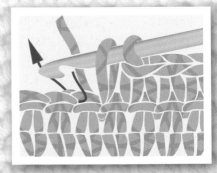
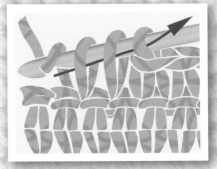
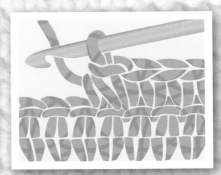

1 Insert your hook into the next stitch, catch the yarn and draw through the loop.

2 Do not complete the stitch, instead insert your hook into the next stitch, catch the yarn and draw through this loop too. You now have 3 loops on your hook.

3 Now, wind your yarn round the nose of your hook and draw through all 3 loops on the hook.

HTR2 TOG or half treble decrease

1 Wind your yarn around the nose of your hook, insert into next stitch, catch the yarn and draw back through 'V' of stitch. You should have 3 loops on your hook.

2 Do not complete the stitch, instead, wind your yarn around the nose of your hook, insert your hook into next stitch, catch the yarn and draw back through 'V' of this stitch. You will have 5 loops on your hook.

3 Finally, wind your hook round the nose of your hook and draw through all 5 loops on the hook.

CHANGING COLOURS

The main thing you need to understand when changing colours during crochet is that you need to use your new strand of colour to complete the last stitch you make in the old colour. It won't seem logical at first but once you've done it, it will all make sense.

Introduce the new colour when you have two loops left on your crochet hook and on the last part of your stitch. Leave a bit of a tail and use the new strand to wind round the nose of the hook and draw it through both loops to complete the stitch. Snip off your old colour and carry on with the new. It's as simple as that.

INTARSIA CROCHET
or colour crochet

If you've done a bit of knitting you will know all about intarsia charts. They work in exactly the same way for crochet. However, there are a few things to keep in mind when working intarsia crochet. Firstly, as you work across the chart towards a colour change, remember to introduce your colour before the change as outlined above.

Also, when using more than one colour in each row you will need to carry the yarn not in use across the wrong side to the point where it is next needed. You can do this in two ways. Firstly, you can strand the yarn loosely across the wrong side of the work. These strands are also known as floats. You must make sure to keep them fairly loose or your work will pucker and refuse to lay flat. This method does not give a very tidy finish to the wrong side of your work but would be fine for something such as a cushion cover. The second method of carrying your un-needed yarn is to lay it across the top of the row and enclosing it within the stitches made with the next colour. Carrying your yarn with you in this way is very neat and the resulting fabric looks similar from both sides.

CROCHETING IN ROUNDS
or in a circle

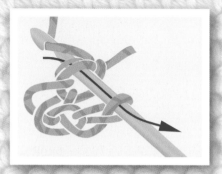

1 Begin by making a ch. In this book I have stuck to 5s, so we will assume the pattern tells you to make 5 chains. Now join the chains to make a ring by making a slip stitch into the first chain.

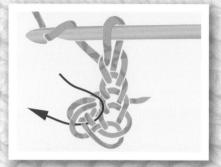

2 The pattern will tell you how many turning chains to make next depending on the stitch you are working. I will assume we are using double crochet so make a 1chain.

3 For the second round, slide the hook under the 'V' of the stitch from the previous round.

4 Now work 9dc directly into the centre of the ring (using the hole as the insert for your hook instead of usual 'V' stitch) and make a slip stitch into the top of the turning chain you made. You now have 10dc in the shape of a circle.

5 Do not turn your work now. Keep working around this edge with the same side of the fabric facing you.

6 Complete each round by making a slip stitch to join the first stitch to the last. If you kept working around and around these 10 stitches, your work would resemble a tube. In order to make it bigger and lie flat, make increases into your following rounds.

RELIEF STITCHES

I have used relief stitches to work a mock rib in this book. At first glance they seem complex but I can assure you they are easy to work and very effective. There are two types of relief stitch used in mock rib:

FRONT POST TREBLE (fptr)

1 Wind the yarn around the nose of your hook as you would in an ordinary treble stitch. Insert your hook around the stem of the stitch below, threading it through the front of the work, around the back of the stitch and finally back out to the front of the work again.

BACK POST TREBLE (bptr)

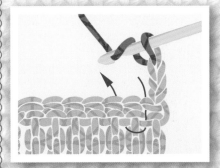

1 Wind your yarn around the nose of your hook as you would in an ordinary treble stitch. Insert your hook around the stem of the stitch below, threading it through the back of the work, around the front of the stitch and finally back out to the back of the work again.

2 Wrap the yarn around the hook and draw the loop back through the work behind the stem of the stitch. You should have three loops on your hook.

3 Complete your treble stitch in the usual way.

2 Wrap the yarn around the hook and draw the loop back through the work so you have three loops on your hook. Complete your treble stitch in the usual way.

finishing touches

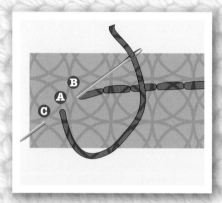

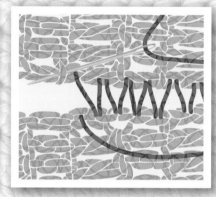

BACK STITCH

Working from right to left. Bring the needle up to right side of work at point A, down at point B and back up at C. Try to keep the distance between stitches even. Begin next stitch at point C. Repeat as required.

CROCHETED BUTTON LOOPS

For an attractive and solid button loop, join yarn at the point where you want the loop to finish. Turn the work and make enough chains for the loop. Miss a few stitches along the edge of your fabric and join the chain to the edge with a slip stitch. Turn the work and work the same amount of double crochet as the chain or slightly more along the length of the loop, finishing with a slip stitch to the edge of fabric at the end of the loop.

MAKING UP USING MATTRESS STITCH

For invisible seams always sew pieces together using matching yarn. Place pieces to be joined side by side on a flat surface with right side facing towards you. Take a threaded needle and secure to fabric by weaving down the side edge of one of the pieces. Bring the needle out between the first and second stitches. Working vertically, bring the needle back up through the opposite piece and insert into first row again from front to back bringing it up below the horizontal strand. Go back to first piece and keep stitching in this way. You will see your stitches form a ladder along the seam. Pull tight every few stitches to close fabric neatly.

DOUBLE CROCHETING SEAMS

This is a fast and easy method of joining seams but it does leave a ridge. You can use this to your advantage and work with it for maximum visual impact by joining the seam with a contrast colour of yarn.

All you need to do is to place the two edges of your crochet together with WS facing. Insert your hook into each of the corresponding stitches along the seam and double crochet into each stitch until the end of the fabric is reached.

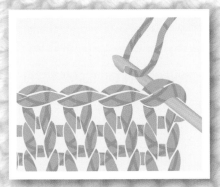  

CROCHET EDGING

With a crochet edging, you will be inserting the crochet hook directly into the crocheted edge of the fabric you are working on.

1 Begin with the right side of the fabric facing you and start at the right-hand corner edge. Insert your hook through the fabric from front to back and as close to the edge as you can. Make a slip stitch by taking your new yarn and wrapping it round the hook from back to front. Now draw the hook back through the fabric towards you with the loop still on it.

2 Wrap the yarn round the hook for a second time and draw the hook through the first loop on the hook. You will be left with just one loop on the hook and your first stitch.

3 Push your hook through the fabric as before and work an even row of double crochet as follows: wrap new yarn round the hook and draw the loop back through your work towards you. You will now have two loops on your hook.

4 Wrap the yarn round the hook once more and draw the hook through both loops. You are now left with only one loop on your hook. This is one double crochet stitch. Continue working in this way until you have worked all around the edge of your garment.

5 Fasten off by breaking the yarn, threading it through your remaining loop and pulling tight.

conversions

GARMENT CARE

After having taking such love and care making your baby's garment, it only follows that you take the same care when washing too. In this way, it should remain looking as fresh and lovely as the day you finished the last stitch.

Always check on the ball band to see which method of washing is recommended for the yarn. For instance, a garment made in 100% pure wool might felt and shrink if washed in the machine at high temperature. In this instance, gentle hand washing might be a better method of cleaning your garment.

However you wash your garment, take care to dry it flat on an absorbent surface such as a towel to soak up excess moisture. Don't be tempted to chuck it in a tumble drier or hang it over a radiator. Dry flat and ease into shape.

CROCHET HOOK CONVERSIONS

UK	Metric	US
14	2mm	B/1
13	2.25mm	–
12	2.5mm	C/2
11	3mm	–
10	3.25mm	D/3
9	3.5mm	E/4
8	4mm	G/6
7	4.5mm	7
6	5mm	H/8
5	5.5mm	I/9
4	6mm	J/10
3	6.5mm	K/10.5
2	7mm	–
0	8mm	L-11
00	9mm	M/N-13
000	10mm	N/P-15

CONVERSION OF TERMS USED

UK	US
Slip stitch	Slip stitch
Double crochet	Single crochet
Half treble	Half double crochet
Treble	Double crochet
Double treble	Triple crochet
Treble treble	Double triple crochet

CONVERSION OF TERMS USED FOR THE TURNING CHAIN

Length of turning chain	UK Stitch	US Stitch
1 chain	Double crochet	Single crochet
2 chain	Half treble	Half double crochet
3 chain	Treble	Double crochet
4 chain	Double treble	Triple crochet

abbreviations

Across	to the end of row		Inc	increase
Alt	alternate		Lp(s)	loop(s)
Approx	approximately		Patt	pattern
Beg	beginning		Rem	remaining
Bet	between		Rep	repeat
Bptr	raised back		Rev	reverse
Ch	chain		RevGrp	reverse group
Ch sp	chain space		Rnd	round
Cont	continue		RS	right side
Dc	double crochet		Sk	skip
Dc2tog	work 2 dc together		Sp(s)	space(s)
Dec	decrease		Ss	slip stitch
Dtr	double treble		St	stitch
Foll	following		T-ch	turning chain
Fptr	raised front		Tog	together
Grp	group		Tr	treble
Htr	half treble		Tr2tog	work 2 trebles together
Htr2tog	work 2 half trebles together		WS	wrong side
In next	sts to be worked into same stitch		Yrh	yarn round hook

suppliers

ARTESANO LTD

28 Mansfield Road
Reading
Berkshire
RG1 6AJ, UK
tel: +44 (0) 118 9503350
e-mail: info@artesanoyarns.co.uk
www.artesanoyarns.co.uk

CORNISH ORGANIC WOOL

Kings Cottage
Boswarthen
Newbridge
Penzance
Cornwall
TR20 8PA, UK
tel: +44 (0)1736 350905
e-mail: info@cornishorganicwool.co.uk
www.cornishorganicwool.co.uk

MARY GOLDBERG Ceramic Buttons

Stockwell Farm
St Dominick
Saltash
Cornwall
PL12 6TF, UK
tel: +44 (0)1579 351035
e-mail: mary@stockwellpottery.co.uk
www.stockwellpottery.co.uk

ROWAN

Green Lane Mill
Holmfirth
West Yorkshire
RD9 2DX, UK
tel: +44 (0)1484 687920
www.knitrowan.com

SIRDAR & HAYFIELD

Sirdar Spinning Ltd
Flanshaw Lane
Alverthorpe
Wakefield
WF2 9ND, UK
tel: +44 (0)1924 369666
fax: +44 (0)1924 290506

SOUTH WEST TRADING COMPANY (SWTC)

918, S Park Lane
Suite 102
Tempe, AZ85281
USA
tel: (866) 794 1818
e-mail: info@soysilk.com
UK stockist: www.angelyarns.co.uk

SUBLIME

Sirdar Spinning Ltd
Flanshaw Lane
Alverthorpe
Wakefield
WF2 9ND, UK
tel: +44 (0)1924 369666
e-mail: Contactus@sublimeyarns.com

acknowledgements

FOR GMC PUBLICATIONS

Photography by Chris Gloag, assisted by Adam Cook.
Flat photography by GMC Publications.
Illustrations by Simon Rodway.
Pattern checking by Gina Alton.

Thanks to the following babies, toddlers and to their mummies and daddies for allowing us to photograph them for this book: Johannes, James, Faith, Bethany, Vermillion, Findon, Alfie, Jack, Charlie, Izabella, Dylan and Ellen.

AUTHOR'S ACKNOWLEDGEMENTS

Thanks must go to Gerrie Purcell at GMC for having the vision to commission this book in the first place. Also, thanks to Virginia Brehaut for excellent editorial skills, Gina Alton for her fine maths brain and pattern checking ability – your attention to detail is outstanding. Also thanks to the guys who made such a wonderful job of the book's styling, artwork and photography.

Special thanks goes to all those who shared enthusiasm for the project and donated yarn and notions. I hope I have done you all proud: Tom Comber of Artesano, Julia and Matt Hopson at Cornish Organic Wool, Mary Goldberg at Stockwell Pottery, Jane Jubb at Sirdar & Hayfield,

A huge, big thanks to Chris Gloag, who took such beautiful photographs. To our cute and wonderful models. We couldn't have done it without you. To Jeff's Auntie Val who stepped in at the eleventh hour and made fire with her crochet hook.

To my ever patient husband and children, Emily, James and Lucy for putting up with woolly talk for months on end and for lending arms to skein wind and untangle said skeins when it all went wrong.

And finally, to Lily; my surprise bundle who started the whole thing yet refused to stay still long enough to try any of it on! May the earth you inherit stay as beautiful as you are.

index

To request a full catalogue of GMC titles, please contact:

GMC Publications Ltd, Castle Place, 166 High Street, Lewes, East Sussex, BN7 1XU, United Kingdom
Tel: 01273 488005 Fax: 01273 402866 www.gmcbooks.com